Team Up

Team Up

Becoming Accountable to your Dreams

Pete Mockaitis

Team Up: Becoming Accountable to Your Dreams
by Pete Mockaitis

Optimality Press
534 W Stratford Place, 10W
Chicago, IL 60657 U.S.A.

Publisher's Cataloging-in-Publication Data

Library of Congress Control Number: 2009933539

Mockaitis, Pete.
  Team up: becoming accountable to your dreams / Pete
Mockaitis.
  p. cm.
  Includes bibliographical references and index.
  ISBN 978-0-9774548-1-5 (alk. paper)
  1. Success—Psychological aspects. 2. Friendship. I. Title.

BF637.S8M366 2009
158.1—dc21

First printing 2009
ISBN: 978-0-9774548-1-5
10 9 8 7 6 5 4 3 2 1

To my accountability partners,
who love me too much to let me remain as I am

Acknowledgements

THIS BOOK WAS REALLY BORN out of the principles it espouses. The mutual support, accountability, and feedback from dozens enrich every printed page. I am so grateful for the generosity of so many. Many contributors even performed multiple duties.

To Connor Danstrom and Jeremy Hewitt, whose frightening invitation sparked this whole adventure. When you do your accountable thing, I have no choice but to get my 10 up. I will treasure our memories and friendship forever. I really, really luh dere.

To all my subsequent accountability partners: Drew Peterson, Jake Vercimak, Avon Fernandes, Jason Buenker, Greg Novak, P.J. Butler, Stephen Mohrman, James Deddens, and Luke Rajlich. I could finish neither this book nor much else without your constant support, encouragement, and feedback. I feel so blessed to have friends like you.

To Professor Steven C. Michael. Thank you for agreeing to support this project so long ago and providing the leveraged guidance that gave birth to the very first draft. Your virtue and wisdom are an inspiration to all who are blessed to enter your classroom and life.

To all my interviewees and elaborate survey respondents (they're a humble bunch, but they can be found in the bibliography). You formed the foundation of this book with your personal content and pointed insights. There is no *Team Up* without your teams' thoughts and innovations.

To the diligent editors who provided rich line-by-line edits: Kristin Barrett, Michael Blackwell, Andrea Hatch, Sarah Roberts, and Lisa Runge. Your attention to detail is greatly appreciated. Thank you for cooperating with crunched timelines and providing your candid feedback.

Acknowledgements (cont.)

To Bobby Deddens, Elizabeth Dickerson, and the gang at Rajlich Studios. Thanks for lending your mastery of photography and barbecue to this work.

To all those who provided rapid, helpful feedback on endless "really quick" questions: Matt Anderson, Shannon Heston, Katharine Johnson, Liz Keane, Janis Kouzmanoff, dave Mockaitis, Anne Pellettieri, Kevin Reifsteck, Emily Retzer, Bradford Schwartz, the Steinman family, Leah Woodard, and assorted Bridgespan ballers plus Facebook friends. I wish I could dedicate a chapter to each of you (e.g. "The Anne Experience"). Instead, I can only offer you my undying gratitude for calming my nerves in the final days.

To Mawi Asgedom. Your mentorship and support have already proven invaluable. I can't wait to see where our collaborations take us in the exciting years ahead.

To two of my all-time idols in authorship: David Allen and Matthew Kelly. Thank you for sharing your wisdom, life, and fame with me.

To master designer Brent "Loops" Jones. You have been the ultimate accountability partner in the final days of this opus. With your raw creativity and patience in processing hundreds of suggestions on the dust jacket and text, you've cemented your place as best-friend-by-sleep-sacrificed and produced a remarkable finished product. Your design and feedback have enhanced this book nearly as much as your friendship has enriched my life.

To Deborrah Shankleton and her talented colleagues at Sheridan Books. Your responsiveness, patience, humor, and professionalism have made our collaboration a joy.

Contents

Rising to the challenge 69

Introduction

WHEN YOU TELL YOUR BOSS you'll do something, how often do you follow through on your commitment? When you make a commitment to yourself, how often do you make good on that promise? If you're like most, your boss gets priority. She has a better chance of getting your attention then you do.

What's that all about?

I've witnessed innumerable personal commitments evolve—and devolve—in a similar pattern. In a moment of motivation, you resolve to undertake an initiative. You name it: exercise, volunteering, budgeting, diet, prayer, study. Despite the inspiration, an inevitable slip of memory, necessary exception, or general sensation of "I don't feel like it" disrupts you. Will you recover? Or will you seek a distraction—some entertainment or easier task to push the failure and its discomfort out of your mind? All too often, we dismiss the resolution and the idealistic notion that inspired us to make it. Whether conscious or subconscious, the message carried by submitting to such setbacks is: "I'm just not built that way; such grandiose visions are beyond me."

Never again.

This book is about responding to the call to greatness each of us hears within ourselves. It's about forging special friendships where you support, admonish, and congratulate each other toward evolving in the most important areas of life. It's about building habits that will enrich and invigorate your whole person and subjugating "I don't feel like it" to truer, higher-level desires. It's about seeing how far you've come, and discovering how much farther you can go.

I've had the great pleasure of witnessing accountable friends use this book's approaches to ensure a broad variety of consistent actions. These consistent actions have led to powerful results. I've seen people start companies, end addictions, write books, and land dream jobs. I've witnessed real dollars saved, pounds lost, courses completed, relationships healed, and spirits lifted. And these victories don't belong to just one person—they belong to the whole team.

However, more exciting than the results are the thrills of progressive personal development and advancements in self-mastery. Dr. Walter Mischel's famous marshmallow test illustrates this point stunningly. In the experiment, a child is presented with a delicious treat and given a choice. The child may eat the treat immediately or he can eat two treats if he waits for a few minutes unobserved. Mischel discovered that, compared to the immediate eaters, the "high delayers" exhibited fewer behavioral problems, formed longer friendships, dealt better with stress, and demonstrated longer attention spans. Additionally, children who successfully waited fifteen minutes averaged 210 additional SAT points over their counterparts who waited thirty seconds. The output of an additional marshmallow matters little compared to the internal strength required to gain that marshmallow.

This book is divided into two halves. The first half, "Our story," tells the true tale of three men struggling with our own discipline breakdowns. It recounts how we stumbled into a way of fortifying each other to achieve previously elusive goals. We were surprised to discover that the process dramatically enhanced our friendships and even transformed the very experience of being alive.

The main characters in this story happen to be male college students who share a dorm and a faith, but the story isn't really about students or college challenges. You might be tempted to distinguish our circumstances as uniquely different from yours. Don't! Just as waiting for the marshmallow means more than double treats, so our ordinary struggles represent more than waking up or being tidy. Our struggles are universal and relevant to anyone who has ever been frustrated by lagging self-discipline. Indeed, people of all sorts across all times have enjoyed powerful results by employing similar principles. As you read the story, I encourage you to empathize with the characters and relate our difficulties to your own.

The second half of the book, "Rising to the challenge," challenges you to commit to a similar journey towards excellence. It draws upon the experiences of other modern-day accountability groups and people throughout history to illustrate the principles that drive success. You'll discover the varied forms that three simple principles—establishing goals, tracking performance, and sharing commitments—can take. The second half's assorted tips and varied approaches will help incorporate the principles into your life. Take the options that work for you and discard the ones that don't. Use it as a reference as you refine your process and adopt new challenges.

You are about to embark upon a wondrous adventure of friendship and self-mastery. Your own adventure will have all the elation, fear, uncertainty, frustration, suspense, and joy of a literary masterpiece. If you accept this book's challenge, you will be astonished at the difference in your life—but the journey is the fun part. Finally, I ask that you share your adventure with me when you're three months into the exploit. Tell me about your glorious struggle, innovations on the process, and amazing results at www.teamupbook.com

Enjoy the ride.

Our story

Frustration

THIS IS A TRUE STORY[1] of conversations transforming lives.

It started with a seemingly innocuous college chat with my friend Connor. At the time, I was a sophomore at the University of Illinois at Urbana-Champaign studying business. I had big dreams of landing a job with a prestigious strategy consulting firm. Meanwhile, I was very slowly progressing on my first book, *The Student Leader's Field Guide*. Connor was a freshman studying biochemistry who considered a career in medical research.

I lived a couple doors down from Connor at Newman Hall, a dorm that grew to become a true home for us while away at college. One spring afternoon, Connor dropped in my room and sat on my bed. He asked, "So, what's happening?"

I sighed as I looked up from my web browser, "Nothing special, yourself?"

"Is everything okay? Why the big sigh?"

"I dunno. I guess I'm just frustrated."

"By what?" Connor asked

"My own lack of motivation, I guess. When the semester started, I was heading up my massive conference…"

Connor put on a giant fake grin and emulated an infomercial: "You mean, Model United Nations Illinois? Illinois' premier United Nations simulation?"

I laughed. "Exactly, you're quite the flatterer. Anyway, I was totally pouring myself into it. So, when it ended, I didn't quite know what to do with myself. Since there was nothing demanding my time, I just did…nothing. Right now, I'm just

---

1. The conversations in this book really happened. When memory permits, the conversations are verbatim records. As odd as our dialogue sounds to many ears, we really did communicate in such a fashion! When memory fails, they are recreated based upon the thrust of the interaction. The names, frustrations, goals, victories, and the peculiar college dude dialect are all very real.

playing around online with no purpose. And lately, I've been sleeping a ton, but I still hit the snooze about five times before I get out of bed. I've been skipping a little more class because it doesn't seem that crucial or urgent that I be there. And I find that more time is being dedicated to Warcraft."

Connor was slightly concerned, "Yeah, those computer games can be bad news."

I shrugged, "Granted, I am decimating my foes with my keen sense of battle strategy…" We both laughed.

"Pete, who says that?"

I agreed, "Yeah, I know. My point is that these little computer game victories are not fulfilling. It's like I've lost that killer, driving instinct to hit my goals."

"Yes. I'm experiencing a little bit of that myself. Midterms are over, but finals haven't quite picked up yet, so I'm just in between."

I jumped up and paced. "I really don't like that in-between stuff! You know, Connor, many students live the whole sleeping ten hours a night, missing class, playing computer game lifestyle and they're perfectly content with it. I'm not because I've seen myself totally on fire, and I don't like slipping into this lethargic state."

"I know what you mean about the on-fire business. I was feeling the fire after this FOCUS [Fellowship of Catholic University Students] conference. Man! Jim Caviezel, *The Passion of the Christ* pre-screening, two thousand solid Catholic students in one spot! I was so pumped up after that. I was praying all the time, hitting up extra Masses, studying in advance of tests, and rocking out in all dimensions. I got up on time, had super productive days, and I was generally high on life."

"Yes! Conferences definitely put me in that mood. Right afterwards, I'm totally pumped up and I get tons of stuff done. It's been that way every time after I hit up my leadership conferences and such."

Connor leaned in, devouring my words. "Yeah, there's something about having all those like-minded people around you that gets it going."

"So, the aspiring consultant in me naturally asks: 'Knowing that, what should we do about our current situation?'"

Connor dug into his biochemistry background and said, "That's hard to say. I mean, entropy is a fact of nature. Nature naturally moves downward to lower energy states. Maybe it's more of a gradual process. I guess as you grow in discipline over time, you are better able to sustain those high-performance levels."

"Ooooh, high-performance, now you're talking my language!"

Connor laughed. "Now that I think about it, I'm thinking that those pumped-up sensations were more fleeting when I was younger, but as I grow more disciplined, I hold onto them longer."

"I see, so you're saying the problem will just take care of itself eventually?"

Connor agreed, "Probably, if you remain vigilant."

I sighed. "Okay, but what should I do right now?"

"I don't know, maybe just play the *Rocky* theme, get yourself pumped up, and do it."

"Or, we should just watch *Rocky*."

Connor agreed, "Sounds like a plan, but which one?"

I snickered, as the answer was obvious.

Connor read my mind as he quickly adopted a Russian accent. He warned, "Okay…but if you suggest a different one, then I must break you."

Rocky IV it was.

Fearful question

WE DIDN'T RESUME THAT CONVERSATION until early September of the following school year. The interim featured Connor and I sharing the shenanigans of college with each other. We returned to Newman room 230 (which became known as "Dirty 230" because of my slob-like tendencies) as roommates the following school year. Connor enjoyed a summer in a research program, growing close to a group of fellow biochemistry enthusiasts, while I matured as a corporate citizen working in marketing for a large corporation. On a nondescript day in September, we returned to a familiar topic.

Connor said, "Man, I was all pumped up to make this semester amazing, and I'm already feeling like skipping classes. It's just like what we were talking about last year when we get all pumped up after an event, and then wimp out later. It's the same thing all over again."

I agreed. "Yes. I've actually been thinking about that quite a bit. It's like we do these conferences and we get all excited—we're rocking out at life, being disciplined, and taking care of business. And then, about two weeks later I'm back to where I was before. Since I typically have about three of these experiences each year, I'm left with six weeks of extreme aliveness and forty-six weeks of sub-optimality."

Connor laughed. "Yeah, that's not a very good ratio, but it sounds just about right."

"No. It sucks," I said. "I remember what you were saying about entropy. I think it's inevitable that we'll fall down to lower energy levels without some force—"

"Excitations if you will," Connor interrupted.

I nodded. "Indeed doctor. Your assertion seems to dictate that excitations are necessary to move us upward. So, I was thinking it'd be nice if there were some manner to self-pump, or create regular pumps in the course of life."

"Oh yeah, keep talking."

"Well, if we just have to accept that we'll drop to lower energy states, then if we increase the frequency of 'excitations,' then the average energy level is higher. That is, if you can frequently create such experiences yourself, then you'll always have at least a little bit of that post-event power."

Connor asked, "Well, that'd be great, but do you really think it's possible to do a self pump-up? The pump-up is really why conferences exist in the first place."

"Well, I think that could be possible. I've been reading some good personal development books lately. I think if you just consistently take particular actions, you will get some of the power that you get from those big conferences and such. The tricky part is taking those actions. It's like I can't stay focused and motivated to do those little things that make a big difference for daily aliveness."

We pondered for a while in the silence…then Connor dropped the bomb.

"Do you think we should hold each other accountable?"

I suddenly felt a gripping heaviness and tightness in my chest. It was that deep-down sensation similar to when I suddenly remembered a previous commitment but really, really didn't want to do it. Strong feelings of obligation and dread descended upon me simultaneously. In my core, I was frightened by the notion. I had a feeling that it would probably work, but would likely be unpleasant.

I was completely honest with him. "Yes…but I'm scared."

Welcome interruption

MY MIND RACED. I had heard the word "accountability" used before—always in a positive context—but always somewhat vague and nondescript. It was a word like "education" that would consistently make an audience's collective head nod emphatically in hearty consent. "Oh yes, accountability = good. Yes." I never did have a clear idea on what the word "accountability" really meant, however.

I pondered Connor's invitation, as our door suddenly flung open. A grinning face greeted us.

"What's up, dudes?!" It was Jeremy, Newman's Head Resident Advisor, senior in business, and all-around hilarious dude. He poked his perpetually silly visage past our doorway. Many Newman second-floor residents had a habit of entering without knocking, but we had bonded such that these entrances were the norm. "I heard you guys chatting, so I thought I'd drop by." Jeremy slid his way into our room, revealing that he was wearing only a blue towel, shower sandals, and a smile.

I smiled back. "Greetings!"

Without giving his minimal dress a second thought, he asked, "So, what's going on?"

Connor replied, "We were just talking about excellence... so I guess the usual."

Jeremy's quick wit engaged, "Oh yeah, right, like when I was hitting on your ladies? That was pretty excellent." Jeremy rapidly looked about, with lips somehow simultaneously pouting and smirking as he raised his hand in search of a high-five. Connor's hand connected in a solid smack.

I continued, "Do you know how you get fired up for a little while, but then it goes away?"

Jeremy agreed, "Definitely. I don't remember how many times I've sworn that I'd get on a consistent running program, but I keep lapsing for this or that or whatever."

Connor said, "We were thinking that holding each other accountable might help with that."

Jeremy grimaced. "Oh, like Big Brother is watching. Yeah, that sounds like a great idea. Commie, you sicken me."

Connor chuckled. "Well, I guess it's something like that. But, I was thinking that, as individuals, we're pretty powerful at rationalizing stuff. It's like you can always make excuses to yourself that you wouldn't make to other people."

"I know what you mean," Jeremy said. "Like, at school, I'm late to class any day of the week. But this summer when I was interning at Nike, I wouldn't dare come in late because the boss-man is watchin'. And I wasn't about to explain to him that I slept for another three hours because I had a sore throat or any of that bull. I showed up every day on time because there was someone watching."

Connor agreed. "Yes, so, it'd be like we would be each other's 'boss-man' in a way."

"Yes!" Jeremy exclaimed. "Why don't we be each other's boss-man? Doing our goals would be like going into work, and we'd have to report to each other."

I could feel my heart rate increasing as I said, "Yes, we could meet regularly, kind of like a 'status report' or update or weekly briefing with the boss."

Jeremy nodded emphatically. "Absolutely. When my boss is expecting stuff done by the weekly report time, I kick it into gear and make sure that I do it. I mean, it's not like I'm going to get fired, but you just don't want to be embarrassed and have to explain why you failed to deliver the goods. I'm pumped! Why don't we do this thing?! Start having to report to the boss-man."

We all exchanged glances. Connor asked, "Well, I'm officially excited…but how exactly will this work?"

Jeremy continued the metaphor, "Well, my boss and I would agree to specific objectives that we believed I could achieve before our next meeting. Then when we met, we'd go right down the list as I provided the status report on each item."

Connor said, "So, we'd first need to establish what the objectives are."

Jeremy agreed, "Right, we'd each need to have our objectives."

I asked, "What should they be?"

Connor suggested, "Well, maybe we can benefit from each other and make recommendations for one another."

Jeremy grinned and said, "So, in other words, we're trash talkin'. I love it! Let's say, five recommendations for each person?" We nodded, agreeing that five seemed reasonable. "When should we start this?"

I said, "Let's start as soon as we can all meet. Also, I was thinking that you don't start a job without an orientation."

Connor said, "Perhaps each of us could orient ourselves with the 'boss-man' upstairs by going to confession."

I jumped up. "Brilliant! Then we can grub right after that and convene."

Jeremy exclaimed, "Whooee! Sounds like we're ready to roll. We'll meet up—is Thursday cool?"

Thursday was indeed cool. It was on.

Kicking off

IN THE DAYS LEADING UP to our first meeting, we bumped into each other and offered additional thoughts for our group's purpose. The anticipation grew and grew. When our meeting day finally arrived, we each had a hearty confession and then regrouped for dinner, exactly as planned. We bounded up the stairs to dear Dirty 230. To say that we were excited would be a major understatement. We were boisterously jumping and joking around, embracing the spirit of adventure in the air. It felt much like the sensations immediately preceding a road trip—but more exciting. A caffeine- and sugar-rich dinner, the graces of some solid confession, and the experience that awaited all combined to create quite a sensation. We engaged in humorous banter for a while and then got down to business.

Connor asked, "I guess it would probably make sense to open in prayer?" We agreed and opened it up, offering thanks and asking for the blessings and graces necessary to make this venture excel.

Connor felt particularly inspired by what he heard moments ago. He said, "Father Tom said something interesting in confession. He cited *The Encyclopedia of Modern Body Building* by Arnold Schwarzenegger."

I shook my head. "That guy is too cool! Who else but Father Tom would reference such literature in confession?"

Connor continued, "I know. But it was really applicable to what we're doing here right now. He said that bodybuilders are tempted to work their biggest, strongest parts because it's just more satisfying and fun for them. Most weightlifters just make a beeline for the bench press. However, the world-class bodybuilders work their weakest parts because they realize that the weakest part is what's holding back their overall development."

Jeremy said, "That's a lot like our class on manufacturing and business process flows. The throughput of a process is limited by the bottleneck. Take a series of machines that transform metal into a finished product. If one of them is really churning through the steel fast, but the next machine doesn't move so fast, then the overall speed at which you can turn out the stuff is limited by the speed of the slowest machine. So, if you make the fast machine faster, it's not really doing anything for you."

"So right now we're working our weak parts and bottlenecks," I said. "The result is that we should build disgustingly huge muscles and churn out thousands of widgets. Awesome!"

Jeremy was anxious to get started. He said, "Alright then, without further ado, let's get into the character assassination, shall we? Pete, I think you're a jerk, and you sicken me!"

I opened up my laptop and said, "Well, since I'm recording all of this and making it all official, I would first like to share my understanding of our group's purpose just to be sure we're completely on the same page."

"Geez, this guy acts like he's writing the book on student leadership or something," Jeremy jabbed.

"He's been writing it forever," Connor said.

I replied, "Yes, mock me. I'll finish it. How about you just take a look at the laptop and tell me if this is an apt summary of all that we have all been saying and thinking about our group's purpose."

I opened up the laptop, which displayed:

Purpose:

- Get things off the "to do list" and into the heart
- Do that sharing and caring stuff
- Become cognizant of how actions affect what you'll say in meetings
- Provide the friendly pressure and bridge to becoming the best we can be
- Provide initial propulsion to start long-term habits
- Conscientiously get past our bull to install habits for a lifetime

Jeremy said, "Sounds good to me! So, if you're done stalling, let's get rolling."

I smirked and continued taking notes with the computer as we furtively unfolded our critiques for each person.

I took a step back to mentally evaluate the situation. I was amazed that this was happening. I knew we were some odd ducks, but seriously: Who has these kinds of conversations? The meta-dialogue goes something like: "Let me tell you what I think is wrong with you." We were about to react by sitting back, taking notes, and thanking each other for the input!

I could feel my heart thumping and my breath shortening as the internal tension mounted. My mind started generating softer language for my critiques.

"So…who's going to start?" Jeremy asked.

I chimed in—quick to postpone my time of reckoning, "I vote Connor, seeing as he's the one who is most disordered."

Connor agreed, "Well, okay, I suppose I can start…but first, how are we going to work this, am I just going to read mine and you can chime in with the ones that I overlooked?"

I suggested, "Why don't we do the reverse, where Jeremy and I speak first? That way, you can see how much our comments match up with what you have. I mean, while I was in the zone of generating faults, I came up with a lot more than five for myself. So, I'd like to first hear which ones jump out at you guys."

Connor agreed, "Sure, either way works. Just bring it on."

Jeremy yelled, "For real, the suspense is killing me!"

I took a deep breath and revealed my thoughts, "Okay, well, I'll just go right down the list. The first thing on my list is drinking. You seem to be able to down many beverages— which is impressive—although also somewhat alarming."

Connor nodded. "I figured that was coming."

I continued, "I suppose we can discuss the particulars of that goal later. Also on my list is being upfront. I mean, people seem to bother you, but you hold it in longer than is necessary. If you address the issues earlier, then you'll experience less stress, frustration, and all that. Also, you tend to be a bit harsh and sort of judge people. If they say something that isn't well reasoned, you relay the tale with an angry tone of voice or throw more blame on them than they're really due. I don't really know how we'd tackle that here. Finally, I think all of us could benefit from regular prayer and exercise. So, that makes five. Whew, I'm done. Your turn Jermz."

Jeremy began, "Right. Well, I concur with young Peter on the drinking. You aren't doing anything embarrassing or anything, but it could get out of hand. Also, I have on here that you should be careful to ensure that you are making time for all your stakeholders—God, your girly, best friends, and peeps who ain't your best friends yet but could be later. I think you could curtail some of the swearing and smutty conversation, and along with that, gossiping or general comments held in ill-will. So, pretty similar to Pete's comments."

Connor remained strong and even seemed uplifted during the course of the character critique. He nodded, paused, and said, "I think you guys are right on. One other item I had is that I think I neglect my family. I'm almost never the one to call. So, should I decide on the goals that I'm going to do now?"

"Maybe," I suggested. "We should let it percolate a bit as we do others' critiques, so you can get additional ideas and/or choose the ones that are weighing heavily on your heart."

Jeremy agreed, "That sounds good. Connor, I've got to hand it to you for taking it like a man."

Connor said, "No, I know it's coming from the heart and that you want what's best for me. It's touching."

"My turn!" Jeremy volunteered.

Connor opened up the volley, "Okay, I'll read my list here. I think I'll open it up likewise with drinking. You seem under control most of the time, but when your friends get together, you get persuaded to drink a couple more than is ideal. Also, your sleeping is all over the place. I've noticed more than one occasion where you planned to wake up at nine, but instead you woke up at one…P.M. Next, from what I've pieced together from your stories, it seems there's room for a bit more chastity in your relationship with the lady friend. It also sounds like your prayer life has been a bit inconsistent. My last one is that you've expressed on several occasions concern that you're cocky. That's it."

Jeremy nodded solemnly. "Excellent analysis, Connor. Peter, what do you have to add to that?"

I responded, "Well, Connor nailed the prayer, waking up, and sleeping bit. In addition to the prayer and exercise that I have for everyone, I only had a couple additional items. First, you have a nasty tendency to use profanities that take the Lord's name in vain and even some ethnic slurs. I know that you're just joking around, and I know you have no hatred in your heart for our Lord or diverse people. All the same, I think that it gives people the wrong impression of you, and it just sounds ugly. My other thing to caution you on is your job search. I know you're in love with Nike from your internship and there's a strong chance that you will procure full-time employment there. So, it makes sense that you're not that motivated to look elsewhere, but I think you need to spend some time shoring up some backup options—just in case. It's like having safety schools when you apply for college."

Jeremy nodded. "Solid performance, gentlemen. I think you hit the nail on the head several times. Thanks for not holding back."

"That's just how we roll!" Connor said, "Now it's Pete's turn."

"I'll start," Jeremy offered.

I braced myself. "I hope you're not too eager."

Jeremy explained, "Well, the room itself is beckoning me to comment. Peter, you are a man committed to living life of, in your words, 'optimality', are you not?"

"Uh huh." I knew where this was going.

Jeremy continued, "This room does not bespeak that at all."

"Word," Connor agreed.

"Just look at this." Jeremy waved his hand about, pointing to the clothing strewn about the floor and the papers jumbled around my bed's headboard. Jeremy's voice grew a bit more uplifting. "When you have an organized workspace, your whole environment supports you in getting your stuff done. Grace builds upon nature, my friend. Make it happen! Next up…Peter Mockaitis, you are an inspiration. You have a lot of really good ideas in that head of yours, and I love hearing your wisdom. You need to share that with the world. Finish writing the dang book! All these student leaders out there are in need of a field guide, and I'm scared that you may let them down. Those are my big two. Other than that, I think you could benefit from prayer, exercise, and getting your homework done in advance. I'm guilty of that too. I think our late night sessions of doing that manufacturing homework should cease. Maybe we can support each other to finish that up in advance."

I appreciated their loving candor. "Thank you. That matches up my assessment of my bottlenecks pretty nicely. Now, Connor: give it to me straight."

Connor dove right in. "Alright, well being your roommate, I would be most appreciative if you would follow Jeremy's advice and stop being a slob. That's probably the one that impacts me the most. Also, I have the privilege of watching your wake up behavior. You are just ridiculous with the snooze button. You can snooze for over an hour! I mean, that's not a very powerful way to start the day. If you really need that extra sleep, set your alarm clock for later. You also seem to be blasted by daytime fatigue. I keep telling you to drink more water to combat that, so that's no surprise to you. You dabble around with prayer and exercise, but I think you could really benefit from an established regimen of that."

I nodded, "Right on. Thank you." A small pause lingered, then I declared, "Whew! Well, I guess that wasn't so hard after all! I had that nervous and excited thing going on, like just before giving a speech."

Jeremy breathed out a sigh and said, "Yeah, not such a big deal at all. So, given all this, what's everyone going to commit to?"

Connor inquired, "Well, how many things do you think we should do at a time?"

Jeremy guessed, "Well, I suppose as many as you think that you can handle. Maybe three to five."

Connor started, "Alright, well, I'll just list the ones that grabbed me the most and you tell me what you think. First, I will pray for one hour every day."

"Dang!" Jeremy and I bellowed in unison.

Connor rejected our praises. "No, it really shouldn't be that big of a deal. I almost do that now, it's just a matter of consistency and keeping it steady."

I replied, "I don't think I could handle an hour of prayer a day."

"You are an impressive dude, Connor," Jeremy said.

"Well, I am rather impressive," Connor said smirking. "But not just for that reason. I'm also going to establish a maximum number of beverages for an evening. I'm trying to figure out what that number should be."

Jeremy asked, "Well, how many does it take before you start being stupid?"

"A lot, maybe nine or ten," Connor replied.

"That is impressive," Jeremy said.

I agreed, "Indeed, you are a machine. Why don't we start out by setting it just below that? So, no more than eight beverages a night?"

Jeremy hesitated. "That works—for now. But I think that eight is already generous and you will probably want to scale it down in the future." Connor nodded, agreeing with Jeremy's prescription.

"What else?" Jeremy asked.

Connor said, "I'm going to return my parents' phone calls every time within the day."

"Solid," I affirmed.

Connor said, "I think that's enough for me. I'd like to really nail these, then expand."

Then, Jeremy began. "You know, one of the big things that I want to commit to, you didn't even bring up—because you don't know that I do it. It goes with the whole spirit of what we're trying to do here. I often just tell people what they want to hear. When people ask me if I want to do stuff, I say that I might, when in fact I have zero intention of doing it at all. So first, and foremost, I want to be completely honest with people all the time and just be straight up and say 'no' when I mean no!"

I chimed in with some scripture, "Let your yes mean yes and your no mean no." (James 5:12)

Jeremy agreed, "That's what I'm talking about! I also want to get the prayer going. I'm going to pray ten minutes at the start of each day and at least acknowledge God's contribution at the end of the day. And I'm going to get going on my relationships. I'm a senior and I've noticed that I haven't ever really bonded with any of the professors here. So, I'm going to initiate conversation with one new professor a week, for about three weeks. Yeah. That should keep me busy."

"Awesome," Connor nodded. "You're up, Pete."

I began, "Well, I've got to say that I'm getting pretty pumped up and feeling some hardcore commitments here. Like an hour of prayer. I hope my resolutions don't seem lame."

Jeremy reassured, "No dude, we all have different strengths; we're here to work on your weak parts, so let's hear 'em!"

Connor agreed, "Yeah, I'm trying to drink fewer than eight drinks a night, so I'm sure they can't sound that lame."

I laughed. "Well, I know I can't get away without some tidiness goal, so…I'll commit to keeping clothes off the floor, bed made, and the shelf above bed clear of everything except immediately necessary reading materials."

"That's a start," Connor said.

I continued, "Next, I'm going to have…twenty minutes of solid, focused prayer time everyday. None of that while walking to class business. I mean real, still silence. I think I can handle twenty for now; maybe bump it up to an hour like the pros later. I'm also going to work on the book for thirty minutes a day."

"Now, is that 30 minutes every day or 210 total minutes in a week?" Jeremy asked.

"Well, I'll try to do it steadily, as in thirty minutes a day, but it's basically 210 total minutes in a week. Finally, I am not allowed to touch the snooze button a fourth time. I must be out of bed by the fourth time the alarm buzzes. Hopefully someday I'll be able to leap out of bed immediately every time."

Connor thanked me, "Your restrained alarm clock behavior is much appreciated."

I wrapped up, "Well, that should be enough to stretch me. Since, we've conducted a thoughtful analysis and we've all set up our commitments, let's do a quick review of the laptop to verify that we're all clear on everybody's goals."

Connor

- Pray every day—one hour a day
- Stick to an eight-drink limit
- Return parents' phone calls within the same day

Jeremy

- Pray ten minutes at the start of day
- Acknowledge God's contribution at end of day
- Initiate conversation—one new person a week for three weeks (professors)
- Be honest—conquer the temptation to white lie every time

Pete

- Keep the bed clear of stuff; keep the floor clear of clothes
- Perform twenty real minutes of focused prayer everyday; check in with God
- Work thirty minutes a day on book
- Never hit the snooze four times in a row

We felt excited about taking on our bottlenecks and tackling some challenging goals. Each of us was ready to rip into them.

Jeremy concluded our meeting. "Well, gentlemen, I think that's quite lovely for a day's work. Man! I'm pumped! Let's go out and show this week who's boss!"

Connor grabbed us. "Definitely, let's rock out. But before we part…shall we close in prayer?"

"Let's do it," I agreed. "And since you have to knock out an hour a day, I think we'll let you do the honors…"

Week 1: First offenses

THE WEEK FOLLOWING the first meeting had a slightly different feel to it. We'd bump into each other and exchange brief dialogues:

"Hey, how'd waking up go today?"

"Solid, no snooze. Did you get the prayer in?"

"Yeah, but I had to skip a shower to do it… stinky!" We checked in with each other frequently, inquiring about each other's performance on the goals. It was refreshing and fun to have the support of Jeremy and Connor and to know that I was providing similar good vibes.

We gathered for our second meeting. Seeing two meetings occur as scheduled boosted my confidence that our little initiative was not going to fizzle out.

Jeremy opened, "Well, it feels good that this meeting with the boss-man is going down as scheduled."

"Indeed," said Connor. "It's already becoming a part of the schedule. Shall we open in prayer? I can take it." We opened it up, joked around a bit, then began speaking of our performance.

I suggested, "I don't know about you guys, but I think the real power is not so much that we are having this meeting now, but just knowing that the meeting is coming down the road. I mean, every time I thought about wimping out on something, I imagined saying to you guys, 'Well, I could have achieved the goal, but I felt a little tired so I took a nap instead.' That just didn't feel right."

Jeremy agreed, "Yeah man, just like we said. The boss-man is watchin'!"

Connor began going over the week, "Well, the eight beverages wasn't really a problem. There was a party on Friday and I kept it at about six and one-third drinks. Prayer was pretty good. I did it most of the time, but I missed it a couple days near the weekend area. I was planning on doing it in the evening, but stuff came up. Once my girlfriend dropped in here, I couldn't really kick her out—not that I wanted to, either."

"I dunno," I said. "I think Jenny might understand that you've made a commitment and have a prayer goal. She might even want to join you."

Connor conceded, "Yeah, you're probably right. More so, she was there and I didn't feel like it."

Jeremy laughed. "I hear that, when my girl is looking all fly, I don't want to send her away, because she might not come back. Know what I'm saying?"

Connor ignored Jeremy, continuing, "So, prayer was generally okay. I was probably just being lazy in some spots. Parents were no problem, so overall I'd say I did pretty well. No complaints."

I congratulated Connor. "Yeah, I think we're impressed that you got about five out of seven days on that full hour of prayer."

Jeremy went next, "Well, I had some really good moments chatting with professors. I set up a meeting with a professor, which went well. The quick morning prayer was fine, no big thing. The honesty was pretty good, but not perfect. But I did have a great session once when Weston asked me if I wanted to join in watching a movie. I really had no interest in watching it, but I said 'maybe.' Later, I went up to him and apologized, saying, 'Look, earlier I said that I might watch the movie with you. I've been striving for a higher level of honesty lately, and the truth of the matter is that, although I love your company, I actually have no interest in seeing that movie. So 'maybe' was a lie. The truth is that I will not be joining you.'"

"Wow! I love it!" I exclaimed.

"Yeah, that's pretty bold, dude. Kudos." Connor replied.

"Waking up, however, was the challenge," said Jeremy, "I usually managed to get ten minutes or close to it with prayer, but the snooze button got me. About half the time I ended up skipping breakfast or a shower or something in order to get it in. Which was not what I had intended at all."

I said, "I can see that. Gaming the system because the boss-man isn't watching the shower or breakfast. Maybe the goal should include that as well. "

Jeremy rebutted, "I don't want to have taking a shower as a goal. That should just be expected. I think I'm just getting into the flow of things."

"Understood," I said. "All the same, it seems that the shower provides an energizing solution that you should seize regularly. One way or another, I'd make that a priority. You could also try portable foods and eat them on your way to class. The cafeteria has these tasty milk and cereal bars, which is what I usually do."

Jeremy agreed, "Good call. Is that all?"

"I think we're done," said Connor. We both nodded.

Jeremy passed the buck. "Peter, that means you're up next!"

I started, "I see! Well, I had a pretty easy time keeping the bed made and clear of stuff. Whenever something was there, it sounded a little alarm bell in my head and I took care of it immediately. It's really a pretty easy thing to do, but it was never a priority until I had set it as a goal."

"I hear you," Jeremy said.

I continued, "Prayer was really good. I felt solid doing it everyday. I realized that I had never really done it everyday with this consistency, so it was lovely…like I'm really getting somewhere. Have you ever watched someone in the chapel and they've all got this angelic stare off in the distance as though they're clearly moved by something?"

Connor nodded.

"Yeah, I feel like I may be beginning to move into that realm."

"Awesome!" Jeremy exclaimed.

"Yeah, that was definitely awesome," I replied. "But working on the book wasn't quite so awesome. I did it about only half of the days."

Jeremy leapt at the chance to joke. He yelled, "You sicken me!"

Connor joined the fun as he earnestly shook his head. "Oh dear, gravely disordered."

"It just got away from me," I said. "I'm not quite sure. I kept thinking that I could make up for it later in the week, but I just didn't."

Jeremy scolded me. "I see. I trust that you'll kick it into gear next week."

Wrapping it up, I said, "Indeed. Finally, I managed to not touch the snooze a 4th time on most days, though it was a bit ridiculous on Friday. I pushed the snooze numerous times. I should have just set the alarm later and indulged in the slumber of class-less Fridays."

"Well, six out of seven is a pretty good start," Connor said. "It was nice hearing your alarm less this week."

Jeremy joked, "Aww, that's so sweet. Roommate consideration."

I finished, "Well, that's it for me! I guess we're done. That wasn't as hard as I thought it would be."

Jeremy said, "Indeed. Perhaps a little too easy."

I grew curious. "What do you mean? Do you think we should be mean to each other?"

Jeremy responded, "No, I'm just saying that when I'm meeting with the boss-man, my objectives are a little more cut and dry. There is a measure associated with what needs to be done and how much I've done. So, I have a solid, quantitative gauge on performance. Like there was a checklist or a certain number of calls to be executed or whatever. I really liked that. Looking at the numbers focused me on what I needed to do. All of us reported our performance in weaker, 'Yeah, I did that mostly, I did some of that.' It doesn't feel like a professional weekly report to the boss-man."

Suddenly a jolt of inspiration struck me that eluded me before. "Wait a minute!" I exclaimed. The words "measure," "objectives," and "weekly" suddenly reminded me of a highly motivating technique I had used before. I couldn't believe that I hadn't thought of it earlier. "So, we've got these goals that need to be accomplished consistently every week, right?"

"Right," Connor and Jeremy agreed in unison.

"And all these goals are essentially 'due' at the same time—the end of the week, right?"

"Yes…" the pair said. I could tell that they were wondering where I was going with this.

I continued, "These conditions are just perfect for a tool I used over winter break to keep me motivated to hit certain goals—particularly working out and progressing on the book. Essentially, it turns your goals into a game where you try to score as many points as possible." I was glad to see them lean forward with interest as I thought that I had struck upon real gold. "Let's see, I've got it on my computer somewhere…"

I sorted through the archives on the laptop to pull up Winter-BreakTrack.xls, an Excel workbook that I had become particularly fond of during winter break of freshman year. I unveiled my creation with gusto.

I could tell that they were slightly overwhelmed by the numerous columns and rows. I attempted to explain, "Each row is a goal I had, and the columns are the days. When I performed something that contributed to the goal, I would put in a number—just a '1' to indicate that I did one workout or a '2' to indicate that I wrote two pages. Then it adds up all the points and divides it by the points desired—so you can see that I worked out eight times, but intended to work out ten times, so I scored an 80% on that goal. It's fun because you can see real progress every day. Then I took an average of the performance across all the goals to see what the overall performance for the break is."

Jeremy enjoyed the solution immediately. "That's cool! So, we could just keep track of our performance on this little guy every week and then report our numbers at the end. I like it. It's a very quantified measure of performance."

Connor asked, "Doesn't that averaging assume that all the goals are equally weighted?"

"I suppose it does," I replied. "But we could go crazy and weight them if we really wanted to."

Jeremy continued, "And since we have quantified performance measures, we can issue incentives based upon that performance."

I loved the way Jeremy's business mind worked. "incentives based on performance" was music to my ears. Connor was more skeptical; he asked, "What, like an ice cream cone? A star for most-improved?"

"I was thinking more like some Steak n Shake." Jeremy explained.

"I love it!" I said. "We can also add some punishments, like a certain number of spankings based upon your percentage, or—"

Connor interrupted, "Now, I don't know if that'd be a punishment for Pete, he's kind of kinky like that, so he might like it."

I shot Connor a look. "Wow! You are out of line!"

"I don't know, you brought it up," Connor joked. "Maybe I don't want to do this accountability thing with you after all."

Jeremy released his signature belly laugh as Connor returned to seriousness. "Well, it sounds like we've got our goals straight and have lots of cool ideas. Why don't we ponder these items and discuss next time. Perhaps we should wrap it up in prayer?"

"Sounds good," Jeremy agreed. "But first, I think that we should issue some assignments. Pete, can you make one of those nifty little sheets for each of us, incorporating our individual goals? And if all of us could think of two rewards and punishment possibilities for the next meeting, that'd be cool."

We concluded our meeting in prayer and began the first week of quantified performance tracking.

Week 2:
The power of numbers

WE GATHERED FOR THE THIRD meeting, opened in prayer, and quickly got down to business. We all seemed to notice a dramatic difference in the way we lived that week. I said, "I don't know about all of you guys, but being 'on the clock' with this spreadsheet really increased my motivation. I mean as I arose each day, points were of the utmost consideration. I had this raw hunger to put points on the board. Did anyone else pick up that vibe?"

"Yeah, I was feeling a little bit of that, but I got distracted here and there," Connor said.

Jeremy agreed, "It was really nifty to have what we in business would call 'key performance indicators' for life itself. But, it's not so forgiving, as you'll see shortly in my score."

Connor chided, "Uh oh!"

"Well, we'll see soon enough," Jeremy replied.

I continued, "It really does remind me of computer games, where I want to get the high score. Except instead of scoring points for mindlessly clicking stuff on a screen, you score them by progressing on your most important life initiatives."

Connor agreed, "Word. That being said, let's get down to business and discuss how our weeks went."

I began. "Well, I can start, I felt pretty good about my week and very motivated by the numbers. Ultimately, I scored a 92%"

Jeremy gushed, "Wow, a 92%! Sweet!"

"Dang dude, that's very nice," agreed Connor.

I appreciated their praise. "Thanks, I feel pretty good about it, but of course I'd like to do better."

Connor rebutted, "No man, 92% is awesome. I was in the seventies."

Jeremy agreed, "Yeah, me too. You are a whole lot of man."

"Wait a minute," I cut them short. "Yes, I feel pretty good about my performance. But shouldn't the standard for excellence be 100%? I mean, I've still fallen short of what I said I would deliver. If we did 92% of what we committed to delivering to the boss, that would not be cause for high praise."

Jeremy agreed, "Yeah, I guess you're right. But then that makes me feel like I really suck."

I countered, "Well, I don't think we should be comparing ourselves with each other really. I mean, our goals are different and the challenge is different for each of us."

Jeremy offered a new perspective. "I think we're just still functioning under the scheme where 90% = A, 80% = B, 70% = C, 60% = D thing. So, I very rarely get C's and feel terrible about my performance when I get them."

"Well, along with that thought, on grades," I replied. "When you receive a paper with a 100%, it feels so much better than getting a 92%. So I really want that!"

"Well, yeah," Connor noted. "But the deck is stacked against us. By definition we chose goals that were previously eluding us. So, it's not fair to expect that your performance on these goals would mirror your academic performance. That's why I'm so impressed."

I blushed. "Well, thank you. It might be fun down the road when we've got a couple weeks under our belt to use past weeks as another point of comparison. Then we can see where we're improving and roll with it."

Jeremy's eyes shifted back-and-forth as though his mind were racing. He suggested, "After a while, we could probably do some cool data analysis on all of this, tracking correlations and all that. It could lead to powerful insights."

"That would be cool some day," I said. "But back to today. Things generally went very well. I missed a day and a half of book writing, and had some snooze challenges. But everything else was perfect. It just felt good. Every day I would look at my spreadsheet and figure out what time I would try and get my stuff done. And it worked out pretty well. Like I said before, the 92% really makes me crave a 100% later."

"Well, I know you don't want to be congratulated," Connor said. "But my hat is still off to you. I don't really feel I can offer any great criticism, since I only had a 73%."

Jeremy challenged Connor. "You should say things regardless. Maybe a fun motto could be, 'Don't just empathize, criticize!'"

"Yeah, that's really uplifting," Connor jabbed.

I sided with Jeremy. "No, but I think he has a point. There's always something that can be done better."

"Okay then, what was the problem with the book?" Connor asked.

I stammered, "Well…I was never really ahead of schedule during the week, I guess there was a little procrastination."

Jeremy replied, "Well, don't do that! Get ahead of pace early on and stay there. It's just more fun that way anyway."

"I think that's really all I have to say," Connor said. "So, if we're all done with Pete, I think I'll go. My performance was much the same as last time, except this time there are hard numbers associated with the performance. 73% sounds really lame, but that's really just a couple slip-ups here or there when you've only got a couple goals. I got some prayer in on the weekend, but not the whole deal. I missed a session that I was planning on doing in the morning. And that's the whole not-so-glorious story."

"Do you schedule in your prayer time?" Jeremy asked.

"I have an intention of doing it at a particular area in the day, like after dinner or in the evening or what-not." Connor replied.

I added, "I'd recommend actually putting it in your schedule. If something's not in my Outlook, it tends to just not get done. So, if you mean business, put it in your schedule. That's all I've got." I said.

Connor apologized, "Well, sorry I let you dudes down, I'll be picking up the pace next time…Jeremy, the one with many goals, how did you perform?"

"Well," Jeremy began. "My performance was pretty similar to Connor's. I had a couple slip-ups here and there that pushed me down to a 71%. I did pretty well initiating some contact with professors and all of that. I think the mornings were the main problem. It was tough to get it all in there."

Connor asked, "Are you getting into bed at a decent hour?"

"Pretty decent on most nights," Jeremy replied.

Connor challenged the assertion. "Now Jeremy, I often see you up at rather late hours, and you just love grabbing grub with Jeff when he gets off his late office shift. For example, this occurred on Thursday night and lo and behold your spreadsheet indicates that Friday morning you did not meet your morning objectives."

"That is true," Jeremy conceded.

Connor continued, "The battle is won at night. If you get into bed at a reasonable hour, it's not too hard to wake up. One way or another, your body needs that sleep. So, if you want to wake up early, you'll need to get in bed earlier to make it happen."

I said, "I agree completely; I couldn't have said it any better myself. Well done, Connor. Actually, I'm going to make that my one and only recommendation for you, Jeremy. Get in bed early. Maybe consider having a bed time. Or find a time where you can take a solid nap without compromising your obligations to compensate for that sleep deprivation."

Jeremy agreed, "That's pretty good. I don't think I want to make a bed time an official goal, but I'm going to bear that in mind and do my best to have the lights out by 1:00 A.M. every night." We found Jeremy's proposal generally agreeable.

Jeremy shifted topics. "Well, if we're all finished with our respective weeks, I'd like to move to our next agenda item. Gentlemen, how did you perform on your assignment to come up with rewards and punishments?"

"Well, I really liked the idea of all of us going out to eat when we get a perfect score," I suggested. "That really motivates us all to support one another. Additionally, if everybody else is performing well, it puts some healthy pressure on the lagging guy, like 'Wow, I don't want to be the guy who prevents us from Steak n Shake.' We could also have some treats—you know, dog training style—when someone gets a 100%. Additionally, I still think that paddles or spankings might be good for punishments."

"Again with the spankings!" Jeremy exclaimed.

Connor replied, "Well, I have some suggestions that aren't so disturbing. First of all, I like the team event thing for those exact reasons. One useful thing for punishments could be pushups. And, because we have these scores summarizing our performance, you can do more pushups if you have a lower score."

Jeremy asked, "So, what would be the ratio?"

Connor suggested, "Well, I think it should be pretty hardcore. I mean, if you got a 50%, you should have to do so many pushups that your arms are in extreme pain the following morning. If you got a 95% it should be fairly easy. I can do about forty pushups consecutively right now, and take breaks to bang out a ton. Perhaps ten pushups per percentage point off of perfection?"

I agreed, "Alright, so with my 92%, I would have to do eighty pushups. That sounds reasonable."

"Let's do it," Jeremy confirmed. "And I think that when someone gets a perfect score we should all celebrate somehow. Maybe doing the slow clap? You know, the silly ending of some movies." Jeremy demonstrated, crescendoing from an infrequent, barely-audible clap until he was jumping up and down, hooting and hollering.

We laughed as Jeremy continued, "Except that two people would be doing the clapping. And, we should perform the applause for each person that gets a 100%. So, if there are two perfect scores in the house, then there are two rounds of applause."

"I don't want to jump the gun, but it sounds like we have a full-blown incentive plan that we're all pretty excited about. We'll do the Steak n Shake run when we all get 100%s, we'll perform a round of applause for each person's 100%, and we'll do a pushup for each 1/10th of a percent off 100% that we get. Sounds great! So, should we all do our pushups right now?"

Connor noted, "I think it would drill our poor performance into our heads and keep the numbers going strong. However, first I wanted to highlight one thing that struck me as we were discussing. I think we're all agreeing that the numbers are cool. Right?"

We nodded.

Connor continued, "Well, I think we are all a bit infatuated with this little innovation, and we jumped right to the numbers in the course of describing our weeks, enjoying the number's extreme summarizing power. But, the number doesn't—and can't—tell the whole story. I think that leaping right to the number can shorten our talk about progress in all of life's endeavors. Sometimes those endeavors will be on the spreadsheet, but other stuff isn't. We should talk about and support each other in those areas as well. That way, we're always up-to-date on what's going on and can provide more understanding of the context from where the numbers emerge."

"Beautiful," Jeremy said.

"You are a wise man," I agreed. "One thing that might be handy to curb that temptation is a little trick we did when I was on staff for my HOBY leadership seminars. After each day, each staff member would quickly list his or her emotional 'high' and 'low' from the day. It was a powerful bonding activity, and I really enjoyed it."

"Well, I think we already basically do that," Connor said. "But having a highs-lows-victories-failures structure in the back of the mind would probably be helpful in curbing the temptation to throw out the number and not share the whole person."

Jeremy replied, "Agreed. Man, that's hot! We are really cooking now. Does anyone else have brilliant insights to share on the process?"

"I'm fresh out," Connor said.

"Well, then, let's get down to the pushups," Jeremy suggested.

Connor stopped us. "Ah, but first, the prayer!"

"Of course, who wants to take it?" I asked.

"I can do it!" Jeremy volunteered. "In the name of the Father, and the Son, and the Holy Spirit. God. Thank you for this delightful week and these fine men. Please continue to support us as we strive to become better men and do Your will ever more faithfully. We ask that you be with us next week and help up grab that 100%. Hail Mary..."

We joined in, "full of grace, the Lord is with thee...."

When the prayer concluded, Jeremy quickly shifted gears. "Now, bring on the pain! I have a feeling that after 290 of these, my score will be improving tremendously next week."

Connor agreed, "Oh yeah."

We got into push up position and counted them off together. "One! Two! Three..."

Weeks 3-5: Time passes as insight grows

AND SUCH WAS THE PATTERN of our meetings. We would open in prayer and each person would share the happenings of the week, reporting on the performance of each goal. Each week we shared our highs, lows, victories, failures, and performance scores with each other. We related with each other's glorious and not-so-glorious moments. Each person would offer different insights on how to power through difficulties.

I remember feeling a bit silly when I referred to a shower as an "energizing solution," or recommended a bed time. However, significant power came from the sum total of sharing all our micro-insights with one another. All the little tips and tricks added up to make a huge difference. Over the course of the meetings, we generated many of them. The author in me captured many bullet points of wisdom on the laptop. Eventually the notes grew to house dozens of handy, memorable nuggets that provided a hodge-podge of useful insights ranging from quick tips to accountability dynamics to human nature:

Quick tips

- When a week is going poorly, use a dramatic mid-course correction. This correction could be a big workout or confession or arising very early.
- Waking up within a minute of when the alarm goes off can yield powerful discipline.
- Pushups in the morning are quite refreshing.
- Rehydration at night and in the morning is very handy.
- Link prayer to other events.
- Get a clothing solution—Use a full-blown hamper. Socks fall out of baskets.
- Write in the morning.

- No matter how early you start the day, you always finish strong. So go ahead and wake up early.

Accountability dynamics

- Ask questions, Socrates-style, rather than yelling or arguing. "Arguments" are for enlightenment—not winning.
- We won't say "forget about it" when another drops the ball. Doing so does each other a disservice.
- In choosing goals, make your spreadsheet fit your week and not vice versa. Exceptionally busy weeks may require a lightened load.
- You feel lousy when you do poorly and great when you do well. The group acts as a lever—amplifying either the positive or negative sensations.
- Look at Excel sheet an appropriate amount—too much means you forget the intent and too little and you lose the desire.
- Be careful at the end of the week; it can slip away.
- Seeing each other being excited produces excitement for all.
- We need our own space. It's hard to have a serious conversation in the cafeteria.

Human nature

- We're only as strong as our bottlenecks / weaknesses. Investing attention in weaknesses is powerful.
- It just doesn't work to be a stud in some respects and a schmuck in others.
- When a desire is only emotional, it's just sappy stuff. When it's a commitment, it's real.
- Going out for "one beer" never happens.
- Procrastination can quietly provide a thrill in the last minute. Deep down inside, steady, structured production isn't as exciting.
- When the project is finally due, you're going wish you had an extra hour. Take that extra hour now.

As the insights bubbled up, we became increasingly interested in our goals and spreadsheets. It was the default topic of conversation. We would come up with different spreadsheet innovations and proudly unveil them to each other.

We would all tinker, until someone made a discovery, which might sound like, "Check this out, it's a pace meter. It calculates the proportion of the week that has elapsed, and then compares it to the amount that you've achieved. The ratio of the achieved to the elapsed is your pace. It estimates the score you'd get if you continued working as you have been. So a pace of 100% could mean that half the week is over and you've achieved half of your goals—so you're exactly on pace."

Meanwhile, Jeremy innovated all sorts of graphical interfaces and fanciful font reformatting. Our conversations had a lingo all their own—like greasemonkeys at a garage or muscleheads at a gym, "Yeah, I got out of class early today, so I was able to knock out some of my goals. It was pretty sweet."

We expanded our rewards and punishment system so that we had to pay a quarter for each percentage point shy of perfection into a communal jar designated for celebrations. So, when someone scored an 80%, that person had to contribute five additional dollars to be used at Steak n Shake.

Amidst the innovation, our second floor neighbors grew more and more intrigued by the activity occurring behind the closed door of Dirty 230. People would knock, enter, and immediately see the focused gaze on all our faces. Often, the visiting party would retract their heads from our door with a "Sorry, Connor, if you could just drop by sometime, that'd be great." Our neighbors would often make references to our "secret meetings."

Week 6: Disappointment

THE QUEST FOR A 100% drove us every week. It was the fifth week of having spreadsheets and none of us had tasted it yet. It became more and more of a primal urge for me. As I arose each day, points were of the utmost consideration. I had a hunger to put points on the board. I thirsted for the perfect score and became flustered when it eluded me. The temptation to cheat was significant, but I managed to restrain myself—most of the time. I found that I needed to make the goals ultra-specific and provide written parameters to reduce any possibility for fuzziness. I was amazed at my own potential for self-delusion.

The most dramatic case of fooling myself involved the cleanliness goal. We had vowed at the last meeting that we were all finally going to get the 100%. Things had been moving along nicely during the week. We were getting close. It was Friday afternoon and none of us had made any mistakes. During a seemingly innocuous roommate conversation, Connor pointed out some extra material on the ledge near my bed.

My mental justification lay ready for articulation. "Oh, I was sick, so I needed to have the tissues and cough drops available there."

Connor persisted, "But what about those glasses of water?"

"Well like mom always says, you also need to drink plenty of fluids when you're sick."

"And those extra books?"

"I've been studying immediately before sleeping, and that's a good place to put them."

Connor was unrelenting, "Yes, but isn't the goal that your headboard shall be free of all materials except your current nighttime reading, notebook, and a glass of water?"

"Well, yeah, but it's evolved since then, considering the circumstances."

"Can you honestly tell me that that's clean?"

He had me.

I was lying to myself all along and I could no longer avoid it. The area above the bed was really a trivial matter, but I felt deep disappointment. I was frustrated that the 100% that I desired was now snatched from my fingers. I was also amazed at how well I could deceive myself. There were clearly items on the ledge above my bed. They had been there for several days, and yet I somehow believed that I earned my "clean" points each of those days. That week none of us achieved the coveted 100%.

Weeks 7-9: Initial tastes

With time, however, we managed to recover the situation. Our frustrations with our inadequacies made us hungrier and hungrier. Meanwhile, the meetings grew more powerful and personal. Nothing was off limits. We would powerfully challenge each other on every aspect of life. We would confront bad attitudes, illogical thought processes, or any action or comment that seemed inappropriate. Our goals evolved as a result.

As we shared more of ourselves in an absolutely honest and caring environment, we grew closer and closer. The process reinforced itself as the closeness we built made us feel even more comfortable sharing and challenging during our exchanges. We ended up hanging out more often outside of the group as well. We would go to the gym or library or chapel together frequently.

Our interactions almost always felt supportive, uplifting, and caring. Few exchanges resulted in significant unease. When they did, we rectified them quickly. Once, Jeremy challenged me on my approach to dating. I was romantically involved with a girl but hesitant to commit myself to an exclusive romantic arrangement. Despite my myriad justifications, Jeremy laid it out, "Pete, that's just bull. You're implying to her 'We're cool now unless something better comes along.' I know that you and her have discussed all that and are in agreement about your status, but it just doesn't seem right. It's a man's duty to protect a woman's heart, and it honestly sickens me." I was pretty quiet during the rest of that meeting.

We didn't bump into each other until two days later, when I saw Jeremy sitting at lunch. Upon my approach, he immediately stood up and we exchanged hearty hugs. He said, "Man, I'm sorry dude. Things just haven't felt quite right between us. I was kinda harsh. I was just saying that because I love you and want you to do the right thing, but I know that you'll do the right thing."

I responded, "No, that's good. Many of the things you were saying were dead on. I just didn't want to believe them. I love you too." Knowing that the feedback came from a loving place made it possible to stomach anything.

Because we lived so close to each other, we had extra information and insight into one another's rationalizations. We challenged each others' excuses. "I didn't have time" was a fun one because we knew each other's recreational endeavors. A typical response to the time excuse might sound like, "Really, that's interesting because you managed to find over four-and-a-half hours to watch *24* in the middle of the week." Over time the excuses disappeared and simple, truthful acknowledgments such as "I'm sorry, boys. I let you down," took their place.

Our enhanced honesty showed up in the spreadsheet scores as they made steady climbs. Excitement levels skyrocketed when individual 100%s started trickling in.

As we first started reaching these perfect weeks, we continued distinguishing the key insights that make the difference between "pretty good weeks" and achieving the flawless victory:

- It started with a firm level of commitment to the goals as worthwhile, high priority objectives.
- From those commitments, a powerful "this shall be" style of determination grew in the gut.
- During the best-performing weeks, we were proactive in taking care of our legitimate needs (sleep, recreation, hydration). We frequently envisioned the moment of triumph and refused to accept the alternative.
- 100% weeks often happened when we were bored with having the same old goals and not accomplishing them. We wanted to set new ones, but knew reaching for more would be illegitimate when we couldn't hit the current bar. We made the push partially just to spice things up.

Fueled by all these factors, our group flourished. Each of us kept adding new goals until our lists were rather lengthy. Each of us more than doubled our initial load of three to four goals. Each week, we felt a little more powerful and capable of achieving our resolutions. We developed a humble confidence in the power of our will. The rapid growth in our relationships and personal power provided an exhilarating thrill that surprised us all.

Our experience of being alive had transformed.

Week 10: Glory

THE FIRST SEMESTER of our accountability adventure raced toward its end. During the elapsed period, each of us had tasted the grandeur of at least a single individual 100% score; however, we still had not achieved the ultimate objective of everyone reaching it during the same week. We were already hardened accountability partners, unabashedly sharing and challenging everything that mattered to one another. It felt good, but underneath the good vibes was a sensation of frustration. Thanksgiving break was looming and our resolve strengthened. The concluding dialogue of that meeting unfolded with a bit more earnestness.

Jeremy rallied, "Okay guys, I think for real this time we can handle this. We're about to have a break, so we can kill ourselves this week and then recuperate during turkey season. We all have a couple tests and papers, but I think we'll be fine."

"I agree, I think that we can pull this off." I said.

Connor forcefully asked, "If not now, when? If not us, who? If not this, what? If not for this purpose, then for what purpose?"

Jeremy giggled. "Connor, you are a hilarious dude. There's also another special item that I've been saving for the end of the meeting. Our dear friend and second-floor fellow Resident Advisor Mr. Drew Peterson has expressed an interest in joining our accountability club."

"Droobie, for real?!" Connor exclaimed.

"Oh boy!" I said.

We were both excited at the notion of adding this extraordinary member to the group. Drew's whole person oozed discipline—from his high school football training, to his excellence in a demanding engineering curriculum, to his consistency at the gym. In our view, Drew was a true man's man. Naturally, the thought of him joining us was exhilarating.

At the same time, we had some reservations. I cracked first, "Man! I love Drew. It would be wonderful to bond with him in this way that accountability does. At the same time, I really want that victory manifest in Steak n Shake. I can feel it in my bones. I know Drew will be a rock star and totally destroy his sheet, but it took each of us a long time to get up to where we were scoring the occasional 100%s. I mean, if you just do the math, it's like each of us has about a 40% chance of getting a 100% score these days. So, the odds that all of us will happen to get it at the same time is 0.4 to the third power or about 6.4%."

"Impressive figuring," Connor said.

"So, if we add a fourth member, that means, by raw numbers, we'd have less than a 3% chance of all getting it together at the same time," I concluded.

Jeremy corrected, "Yes, but the numbers aren't independent like that. When we really decide to kick it in as a group, there's a much better chance."

I conceded, "I know, I know. The numbers aren't perfect, but the main point is that adding a fourth person will make it really, really, really hard for everyone to get a 100% at the same time."

"All the more reason for us to kick it in hard core and get the job done this week," Jeremy replied.

Connor summarized, "Right. This will put some good pressure on us to get it done. We know it will be harder with four people and may not happen before Jeremy and Drew graduate. So, that powerful, urgent 'now or never' effect could be just the push we need."

"Great observation, Connor," Jeremy said. "So, let's get to it! We're going to dominate this week. Let's show Drew what men he's getting involved with. We're not little pansies. We're victors! And once we're victorious, we'll bring him along on the Steak n Shake adventure and give him a real taste of what this is all about!"

We parted with a unique enthusiasm. Following the meeting, the commitment and determination remained strong. Something was different this time. The power of being accountable to each other was amplified by the supreme importance of achieving this victory. We each envisioned the glory and checked in with each other multiple times a day to ensure that we were on track. As the week grew closer and closer to being over, it became clear that we were really going to pull it off. We were overcome by excitement.

The revelry on the evening of our victory was quite a scene.

Moments after we completed our final points, each of us entered Dirty 230 with shouts of "Yeaaaah!" "Booyah!" and "Victory!" We jumped about the room while playing assorted hip hop and dance tracks, busting out ridiculous dance moves and making goofy faces while doing so.

Jeremy summarized, "So, three 100%s means three rounds of applause, right?"

We engaged in three rounds of boisterous, growing applause. After calming slightly, we picked up Drew to depart for Steak n Shake. Fortunately, Drew was unreserved, feeding off of our enthusiasm and jumping right into the fun. The dancing and hilarity from the room spilled over into the Jeep. Connor managed to keep steady control of the vehicle throughout all of our shenanigans.

The ride was swift but joyous. We would yell items such as, "Hey! We all got 100%!" to the pedestrians as we passed. We pulled into the Steak n Shake parking and scurried into the eatery like a high school football team rowdily celebrating their victory.

At the restaurant, the waitress seated us and could sense from our ebullience that this was an event. We boldly informed the waitress that we were celebrating. Although she clearly had no idea what we were talking about, we attempted to explain "You see, we all got a 100%. That's the first time that's happened in ten weeks!"

The waitress clearly felt a bit awkward about our energy. "Well… congratulations," she mustered. I imagined that the Steak n Shake staff had probably seen worse from miscellaneous late-night drunkards, so I didn't feel too bad about it. We laughed throughout the ordering and waiting process.

I commented on the ordering. "Man, it feels extra good knowing this will be paid for with the accountability funds. You know, when you're really victorious, it feels like someone else should be paying for it. And by golly, someone else is paying for it. Our treasury is doing its work."

When the food arrived, Jeremy unabashedly led us in prayer, "Thank you, dear Lord for this glorious victory that we're sharing together. Thank you for Drew coming to join the fun and being with us throughout this long journey. Stay with us during our time of joy and bless this wonderful food. We love You."

We settled a bit amongst the chewing and slurping. During the temporary calm, we spoke a bit about what had made the difference this week.

I said, "I didn't want to be the guy who said, 'Sorry, I failed, so we can't go to Steak n Shake.' I'd not only be ruining it for the three of us, but also for Drew, who wants to join up with this posse. That's just not cool."

Connor agreed, "I guess it's really not that hard, which is weird, seeing as it took so long to get here. I mean, when you decide that this is what you're really going to do, then you make it happen. It becomes your priority and all other opportunities and options take a back seat to this."

"Yes!" Jeremy resonated. "I mean, in other weeks, opportunities to chill with people, hang out, have a good time had more allure than they did during this week. This time I was just like, 'No way! That might keep me from getting my 100%. You can forget about it.'"

Connor elaborated, "The pressure that we offer each other every week really got kicked up a notch because the stakes were higher. So, it was easier to stave off temptations. The alternatives just don't compare."

"So," I said. "It seems there's a difference between being committed and really being committed. I mean, I think I've learned this lesson before, while working within student organizations. When you're ready to sacrifice fun, sleep, and even grades—that's when you know that nothing will stop you."

"Well, I can see that's true," Connor replied. "But what makes this moment special and different is the team atmosphere. I mean, my victory is great and all, but it's the team thing that makes it awesome. I feel as great about you two dudes getting your 100% as I do about my own. And we did it as a team, each supporting each other. It's just a beautiful thing."

"Right on," Jeremy agreed.

All the while, Drew sat back with a smirk on his stubbled face. He was soaking up the joy of the experience.

Jeremy asked, "So, Drew, you think you want a piece of this?"

Drew didn't hesitate a second. "For sure!"

Jeremy laughed. "I knew you did—grinning over there. I just wanted to hear you say it!"

Drew offered up a toast with a milkshake. "I just wanted to say to you dudes, that I really admire how you've grown this semester. It's extraordinary. Jeremy, you've taken on the responsibilities of Head RA like a real man. Connor, you have picked up so much discipline. And Pete, I don't know if you knew Christ before, but I can totally see that you know Him now. It's really a beautiful thing. I'm honored that you're letting me join you, and I really look forward to growing with you men as an accountability partner in the weeks ahead and getting what you guys are getting out of this."

As we absorbed Drew's warm words, all three of us were struck by a bout of eye moisture. Jeremy said, "Drew, I speak for all of us when I say that we are the ones honored by you joining our group. I can't wait to learn from you and get a piece of what you have going on."

We lifted our glasses and cheered for Drew.

When we wrapped up our evening, we actually enjoyed paying the check, for two reasons. First, it felt like someone else was paying. Secondly, it was cathartic to see all the quarters we accumulated—representing our failures—be exchanged for our victory celebration.

The whole experience was surreal. As I fell onto my bed from exhaustion, I felt a satisfaction so glorious. We had achieved our mission. We were bringing another man into the group. I greatly looked forward to next semester. With all this discipline assimilated, I knew we could do extraordinary things. We would hit the ground running powerfully. I crossed into slumber with visions of victory dancing in my head.

That was one of the best night's sleep I have ever had.

Weeks 11-13: The Drew experience

JUST AS WE EXPECTED, Drew was an accountability power-house. He started with a healthy load of goals and his initial scores still put ours to shame. He always scored in the nineties. He would use strict accounting standards—giving himself zero points if he didn't accomplish the full goal. He offered us power-ful, no-nonsense advice and illuminated pieces of our Catholic faith. He got us started solidly with the rosary and explained the small piece of cloth he wore around his neck—a scapular. He also gave us many valuable pointers on weightlifting technique.

Having an additional person to provide his support and in-sight really enhanced the accountability process; however, such gains weren't free. We discovered that having another person's week to analyze resulted in longer meetings. We had to schedule longer blocks of time or curtail some of the tom-foolery and shenanigans.

Drew's hardcore approach manifested itself in many ways. In the second week he said, "Guys, I'm bumping up my workout goal to four times a week."

Jeremy asked, "Are you sure that's really optimal? Are you just trying to make it tougher?"

Drew replied, "No, actually, I wanted it to be four initially, but I thought I would start easy with three just to be safe so I don't turn in a bad score." The rest of us only had two or three work-outs on our sheets, so we were impressed. Every week he made one of his goals more challenging or added an additional goal.

As a matter of fact, Drew made it look a little too easy. Once Drew turned in another supra-95% performance despite endur-ing some romantic difficulties. Connor suggested, "Drew, you're dominating these goals so hard, you may be capable of more. I'm not sure if you're learning as much as you can be."

"What do you mean?" Drew asked.

Connor continued, "Well, I think the three of us learn by trying really hard, screwing up, and then learning from those screw-ups."

"Are you saying that you want me to screw up on purpose?"

"No, I'm just saying that you might want to make your set of goals a little more challenging."

"I think it's pretty challenging. I mean, I'm adding something new every week."

Connor concluded, "I know, but it's just something to think about."

Drew was rather quiet for the rest of the meeting. We worried that perhaps we had offended him.

Extending dude-hood

ANY WORRIES ABOUT OFFENDING DREW disappeared after we were invited to present our accountability concept at an event for FOCUS, a Catholic ministry on campus. The event consisted of a barbecue and a speech...and we were the speakers! It was the first time that we had shared our story with a broad audience. That day, we prepared our presentation by dividing the material into four segments. As I prepared the spreadsheet handouts, I imagined just how powerfully this could impact the twenty students gathered at the occasion. We were about to summarize the whole process.

As the feasting approached its conclusion, one of the hosts provided a simple introduction. "These guys are going to do a little presentation on their accountability club, so if you could kindly direct your attention to them, that'd be great."

We situated ourselves, distributed the handouts and prepared to begin. Matt, a statistics major, immediately noted a zero at the intersection of Friday and a "hypothetical" drinking goal represented in the handout. He called out, "Someone had some fun on October 11th" to open us up with a good laugh.

The conversation flowed very naturally as we summarized our relationship, our story, and our process. As we got a chance to reflect upon our adventure together, each member brought new items to light. The audience responded to a few points in particular, highlighted here.

Jeremy said, "When Connor and I started this, we had something of a strained relationship, with some back-talking and gossip. But now, it shows a whole new level of friendship, when you have the guts to call a friend out on doing something stupid. It's a powerful thing. I also notice that you put up with people's bull a little less. You find yourself speaking up a little more often, and it makes a difference. You find yourself demanding excellence from other people, and if you give them a chance, they produce. That's what I'm finding."

"Sometimes," Drew added. "When there's something really tough and personal, my confessor tells me to bring it to accountability. And sometimes I was like, 'Yeah right; I'm not telling these dudes these things…'" The audience laughed.

Drew continued, "But afterwards, I'm glad I did. There are things on my goal sheet that I probably wouldn't do if they weren't on there. I probably wouldn't work out four times a week. I love it, and I love it when I do it, but I wouldn't do it if it weren't a goal on there. I wouldn't pray as long as I do if it weren't a goal. But when you have three guys there, you're just afraid of showing up to the Sunday meeting where they are going to say, 'You are a sap. Get your act in gear,' it makes you want to step up."

Heads nodded in reassurance as Connor added, "Another cool thing is that when you open up to some guys that you trust and get feedback, it makes it so you don't want to have any more deep, dark, secrets. It starts fading out of your life because you don't want to be having any stuff like that, if you're going to be verbalizing it. Exposing yourself to the light is a powerful, scary thing, but it's not so bad when you do it on a small scale."

I said, "I find that I'm more honest in my groups and projects. When I've failed to deliver something I said that I would, I now admit it honestly, rather than try to skirt around the issue like I used to. By honestly acknowledging that I screwed up and receiving forgiveness, I can tell that I'm respected more by my group members and it makes us all more comfortable with requesting that people do what they say they will."

Father Tom asked, "So how do you start?"

Drew joked, "Well, there's an activation fee of $19.95, but if you buy now—"

"—You'll get a free spatula," Connor finished. "Well, this organically happened as a part of our friendship following a natural conversation along these lines. So we had a good starting point there. I say just ask your friends—here or elsewhere—who want to be better, because I think we all do. Once you get rolling, you don't want to stop. And if you do want to stop, there's somebody there telling you not to. I'd say approach one or two people and see what they think. I doubt you'll get a 'no', most people will just be scared."

An audience member asked, "I guess one of the issues with this is that you might become rigid and judgmental with things. What do you do about that?"

"Actually," Jeremy replied. "I've just noticed the opposite. For example, Connor—I mean, someone—in the group had an objective of drinking fewer than eight drinks in an evening, and one of mine was twenty minutes of prayer. And, the goal of less than eight drinks seemed pretty ridiculous to me, but that same someone was doing an hour of prayer a day. Even within the group there's a temptation to want to judge wimpy goals. But now it's not a source of judgment, but rather inspiration. Now, instead of yakking about how that person has a tough time drinking fewer than eight drinks, I want to help that person. I mean, everybody's different, which is something I've realized through this. Everyone struggles with different stuff. My struggles may seem ridiculous to someone else and vice versa."

We mingled with the group and it was exciting to see them intrigued and asking questions. I recorded the whole talk, which I occasionally revisit in bouts of reminiscing. The recording reminds me of our enthusiasm, our fumbles, and our purpose. It's an inspirational snapshot of the closeness and discipline that emerged in just a couple months.

Going forth

OUR EVENING MEETING following the barbecue felt really good. We had shared our concept with the world and gathered some favorable responses. A few people had already started their groups. Little did we know that the growth had just begun.

As Drew concluded reporting his performance he said, "On an administrative note…" I settled into a comfortable thinking routine as I thought, "Ah, administrative notes, Drew probably has a test or something during the next meeting time." But Drew's note contained much more.

Drew continued, "I've enjoyed my weeks with this accountability group, but I will no longer be participating."

Jeremy, Connor and I were aghast. We shot each other looks.

Connor said, "Hey, Drew, I hope this doesn't have anything to do with that talk about failing on your accountability sheets. I mean, I was doing a lot of thinking—"

Drew interrupted, "I pondered those words for some time—"

"No," Connor interjected. "I was thinking, you probably are just really that hardcore. I mean, you make a lot of sacrifices to perform well on accountability stuff, and what I said didn't respect that. It's like a slap in the face, and I'm really sorry."

"Well yes, that hurt," Drew replied. "I do make real sacrifices—leaving parties early and that sort of thing. So when I come to the meetings, I expect high fives, not to be kicked down."

"Oh man, I'm so sorry," Connor apologized.

"I forgive you. Thank you for explaining yourself and apologizing. We're cool."

Jeremy asked, "So, then are you going to stay with us?"

Drew said, "Well, that's not really the reason that I'm leaving. It's Jeff and Dave."

"Jeff and Dave?" I asked. They were two other floor mates and two of Jeremy's best friends. We were puzzled.

"Well," Drew explained. "I keep seeing them pop their heads in here when we're doing our meetings, and every time they seem disappointed when they have to leave. I sensed that they might want a piece of the action. So, we talked, and we thought it'd be great to start a group of our own."

"Well, it's cool that you're getting them involved in the action, but I'm really going to miss you," Jeremy said.

"Well, it's not like I'm dead! I'm still just five doors down. We'll be hanging out all the time. Besides, the three of you have your group established and I was always the fourth wheel...if that makes sense?"

"Drew, you were a great addition," I said. "We loved having you."

Drew nodded. "Thank you. I've been praying about this and I really believe it's the right thing to do."

"Well then, I don't want to get in the way of progress. I wish you the very best with your group," Connor congratulated.

"Yeah man, I really valued your contribution," I said. "I'm praying the rosary every day because of you."

"I'm in agreement with these gentlemen," Jeremy said. "I love your presence in our group, but can see that you may be called to higher things. Given that, perhaps there should be some ceremony commemorating our times together."

Drew suggested, "Well, we could pray a rosary together."

"Let's make it a walking rosary on the quad," Connor recommended. "That feels ceremonial."

And so the four of us grabbed our rosaries, headed out to the quad, and strolled side-by-side as we prayed the beads. I felt so grateful that I had the opportunity to be enriched by these men and so proud that I played a role in their enrichment. The evening concluded with big hugs for Drew. In a little way, the sensation in my stomach was similar to when someone moves away. I knew that I would miss sharing particular experiences with him, but welcome the exciting new opportunities awaiting him.

Renewal

"I miss Droobie."

Exactly two weeks had passed since Drew's departure announcement. Our disappointment had diminished a bit as we heard about Drew's new accountability partners' enthusiasm and initial victories. Jeremy, Connor, and I continued our mutual optimization, but it just wasn't the same; we found that returning to three provided for more efficient meetings but less insight. However, having tried accountability a couple different ways and watching it spread inspired us. The dreamer inside me began fantasizing about how the concept could work for any set of friends who aspire to excellence. Accountability might appeal to an audience much broader than four odd college dudes with an infatuation with "racking up points" on an Excel spreadsheet.

On a lazy Sunday afternoon amid such ruminations, Connor and I were enjoying some midday chilling in our room when a rap at the door summoned our attention.

"Enter!" I beckoned.

The face emerging from the doorway belonged to Jake. He lived just three doors down the hallway. Jake was a pale, tall, and skinny fellow with a perennially toothy grin plastered about his face. However, most Newman residents probably knew Jake as the guy who hauled a gargantuan glass mug of Mountain Dew from the cafeteria to his room. The second-floor men knew the other side of the story. Jake would consume the entire mug over the course of a late-night chemistry studying session. After studying the whole night, he would later catch up with a thirteen-hour sleep bender the following night. It was an odd ritual—and one we often reminded him might not ideally facilitate absorbing chemistry content.

Today his smirk seemed particularly acute. He seemed to be sneakily planning something. I was intrigued.

"Greetings," he said. "I had a session with one Father Tom, who had many interesting things to share."

"Do tell," Connor encouraged.

"He recommended that I see you two." I had never had a referral from a priest before, so I was flattered but puzzled. My intrigue mounted as he continued, "He informed me that you may have something rather valuable to share for my situation."

Unsure as to his intentions, I inserted some consulting babble. "Hmmm, I do aspire to provide a variety of integrated solutions, so could you be more specific?"

Jake continued, "He spoke of… a unique system that you gentlemen had used that proved rather valuable."

Jake's smirk was now officially mutual. I could feel a grin growing bigger on my face; looking at Connor, it was clear he also felt the vibe. We tried to contain our excitement. If Jake was pondering what we thought he was pondering, he had no idea what kind of the thrill ride awaited him.

I coolly inquired, "What system do you mean?"

His coy attitude was signature. "A little something to do with goals and spreadsheets and optimization."

"Oh… I think I know what you mean," Connor said.

Suddenly, Drew's departure seemed like a blessing. It was an opportunity to take another friendship to the next level. A chance to bring some structure into the life of a binge sleeper. An opening to begin the adventure anew.

I summoned Jake over to my laptop. Excel was open and the ubiquitous PeteSheet awaited its exhibition. The conversation seemed pregnant with significance: "Each row is a goal that we've set for ourselves, while the columns represent the day of the week…"

Jake's eyes grew wide with wonder. His questions clearly indicated that he was hooked.

We could hardly wait to tell Jeremy...

Rising to the challenge

Your turn

AT THIS POINT, IT'S EASY to say that this was a fun little story[2] while tucking this book away with a weak intention of returning to the rest of it some day. Unfortunately, such an action would make both of us losers. My mission in sharing the tale of Pete, Connor, Jeremy, and Drew (hereunto referred to as "The Dudes") is to provide inspiration towards action. I hope that the accountability adventure you just read foreshadows your own trek toward becoming accountable to your dreams. Integrating some extra accountability into life has proven powerful for many beyond just The Dudes…and you're next!

You may say, "This seems neat and all, but I don't really think that it's right for me." Fortunately, the remaining pages make it easy to mix and match components of accountability to help it fit your life.

If you have reservations, they could stem from fear rather than reason. Forgive my presumption, but one way or another, your life can probably benefit from some accountability. Connor puts it even more forcefully, "If you think you can assimilate virtue and conquer 'I don't feel like it' without a little help from your friends, you're not only wrong, but misguided and pompous." So please stick around for a few more pages before putting this book aside.

Holding back

It's natural to have some initial resistance to jumping into an accountability challenge. Indeed, my initial response to Connor's invitation was "Yes, but I'm scared." You might be terrified to expose such tender pieces of yourself. You might not like what you discover about yourself or your friends. You might experience some tense moments. You might feel demoralized by repeated failures. Sounds great!

2 Another understandable reaction may be, "But what happened to the dudes?" Short answer: Great things…but the answer is still unfolding because we're still alive! You can visit www.teamupbook.com to learn more.

In life, everything has a cost. During my speaking engagements I'm fond of saying, "*The Price is Right* is not merely a means of passing the time on a sick day, but a profound universal truth." Everything in life has a price tag. Enhanced friendships, personal victories, self-mastery, and the pride of progress are not free. Enjoying such gains in an accountability context requires courage, trust, and time. You will probably endure some fearful, unnatural, and unpleasant moments. Is it worth it? I dare you to find out!

Defying your fears is one of the most thrilling experiences under the sun. Why is skydiving so much fun? Because it's terrifying; there is an element of risk. You could say the same of public speaking, gambling, and dating! The accountability thrill is similar. Your internal opposition may sound something like:

- "I'm going to have to change everything about myself."
- "I just don't talk about these things with people."
- "I don't want to make my current friendships all uncomfortable with that yucky stuff."
- "Can I really trust these people with this stuff?"
- "You can't teach an old dog new tricks."
- "I get harassed enough by my boss and spouse; I don't need any more."
- "I don't want to live my whole life based on numbers."

Let's balance the risks with the rewards. Here's what a few accountability people have to say about their accountability challenge:

- "My favorite part has been seeing my accountability partners become the better people they have always wanted to be. I am very proud of them. I think that we will be united forever." -Alexandra
- "[I am] finally realizing that life is worth living when one rises in the morning thankful for a new day as opposed to wondering how you will get through it long enough to go back to bed." - Jason

- "These people will be a different type of friend forever."
  - Jeremy
- "This could be the single best thing I learned."
  - Greg

Whatever your concerns, others have had them and discovered value in applying the principles of accountability. Ask a few people if they could get excited about this. As you'll learn later, these people could even be strangers.

Infinite variations on three principles

You can unlock similar magic in your life whether or not you follow the regimented approach of The Dudes. The particulars of our group may not be your cup of tea. Spreadsheets, push-ups, Steak n Shake—such trinkets may or may not gel with your friends, goals, or approach. Fortunately, this second part of this book provides glimpses across the broad universe of personal accountability.

It turns out that The Dudes weren't the first—or the last—people to apply similar principles to incorporate discipline. From ancient philosophers to Web 2.0 applications, team-based approaches to living the good life have flourished throughout the ages. You'll read a little about them all to provide inspirations for designing your own accountability masterpiece.

The second half of this book also draws upon the experience of numerous other individuals who have tackled accountability in a structured group setting similar to that of The Dudes. Twenty-four people generously provided in-depth input on what goes on inside their accountability groups. So, when you see a random first name appear (e.g. "Laura recommends") that comes from someone recounting his or her personal accountability experience.

The principles behind The Dudes' accountability complement universal human tendencies and difficulties. Similarly, other accountability approaches all employ three simple principles. These principles are helpful to anyone who has ever been a friend or a failure. They transcend the experience of any one group. They are:

I.   Establishing goals

II.   Tracking performance

III.   Sharing commitments

I. Establishing goals

It all starts with an aspiration. This section will provide some key tips to help you identify goals and build good habits as you delve into an accountability process. In particular, it will look at four areas of your life to highlight powerful—yet often overlooked—goals that can quickly make a huge impact on your life. The section will also provide tips and tricks for making the goals trackable for the rest of the process.

II. Tracking performance

The Dudes had an infatuation with data—as indicated by the elaborate Excel spreadsheets. Whether or not spreadsheets are your thing, tracking progress proves an essential and highly motivating element of any accountability benefit. In this section you will find goal tracking options and tips as old school as Benjamin Franklin and as modern as Web 2.0.

III. Sharing commitments

Sharing your deepest aspirations and concerns in life brings people together on a whole new level. The men in the story had an initial respect and admiration for each other, and they dramatically enhanced it by regularly talking about their highest priorities. You can initiate these conversations by being a catalyst armed with this book. This section of the book will provide guidance on how to pick your co-adventurers toward greatness. You'll learn from the successes and mishaps of other accountability folks in identifying the best humans for the purpose. Then, you'll see how people kept the relationships growing stronger during the inevitable tensions that emerge.

Additionally, you can apply these three principles in either a "light" or "heavy" fashion. Consider the following chart:

Principle	Light	Medium	Heavy
Establishing goals	Tackling stuff you just need to get done (e.g. that postponed project)	Addressing a key area of your life (e.g. fitness, finances)	Installing habits that will transform your whole person
Tracking performance	Life wish lists	Goal action plans	Integrated, daily aspirations tracking
Sharing commitments	Telling strangers on the internet	Making bets with co-workers	Sharing your whole life with trusted partners regularly

While you'll reap a greater reward for "heavier" investment in accountability, pick what works for you...and enjoy the ride! As a bonus, the fourth and final section reflects on the magic and mystery of the accountability lifestyle.

An abbreviated history of personal accountability

ACCOUNTABILITY HAS BEEN GOING STRONG for many, many years. Take some inspiration from how different people have enjoyed the benefits throughout the ages.

The ancient Greeks

Around 500 BC, Pythagoras (famous for his theorem on the hypotenuse in triangles) was one of several philosophers who lived in community with his disciples. Their followers shared a commitment to seeking truth by following the disciplines of the community. The disciples practiced a wide array of fascinating rituals designed to help them excel in the art of living. For example, new Pythagoreans entering the community would remain silent for five years in order to master listening and thereby absorbing the wisdom of the masters. Additionally, disciples would nightly examine their lives and the actions of the day prior to going to sleep.

John Wesley's "holy clubs"

In the early 18th century, Christian theologian John Wesley formed a spiritual accountability club while studying at Oxford University. Wesley's compatriots gathered regularly, whereupon each individual would provide truthful answers to a list of over twenty hard-hitting questions. The list included questions such as "Am I a hypocrite? Am I proud? Do I grumble or complain constantly? Did the Bible live in me today? Am I jealous, impure, critical, irritable, touchy or distrustful?"

Alcoholics Anonymous

In 1935, Bill Wilson and Dr. Bob Smith teamed up to found Alcoholics Anonymous. Now, over two million people participate in AA at over one hundred thousand groups. Group members share a common goal: to become and remain sober. Members share their experiences with each other at the group level and more personally at the sponsor level. Newer members find experienced members who help them follow AA's famous twelve steps. The accountability present with the sponsor helps both the sponsor and the newer member remain sober.

The Master Mind group

In 1937, Napoleon Hill published a self-help blockbuster that is still reprinted to this day, *Think and Grow Rich*. In it, he shares perspectives on accumulating wealth through positive thought and action. Perhaps his most famous advice is to convene a "Master Mind group." Such groups meet in person, twice a week, in a "spirit of harmony" toward a "definite purpose." Each member was to clearly articulate his specific desires—and all members were to brainstorm actions and hold each other accountable to performing those actions.

Weight Watchers

In 1961, an overweight Jean Nidetch enjoyed a little weight-loss success at a free diet clinic sponsored by the city of New York. But when she began losing motivation, Jean turned to her friends. "I realized that what I needed was someone to talk to who could give me some feedback…And if I needed it, others needed it just as much," she shared with the Horatio Alger Association. From this mutual feedback evolved a regular, weekly meeting that featured weight goal setting and check-ins. They supportively shared the highs, lows, victories, and failures associated with progressing against their weight goals. Employing these accountability principles, Nidetch lost over seventy pounds. Following this victory, she incorporated Weight Watchers, which has since grown to reach nearly forty million participants and generate billions in annual revenue.

www.stickk.com

Founded in 2007, stickK enables you to "put a contract out on yourself" (the additional K is short for "contract" in legal lingo). Dean Karlan, stickK Co-founder and Assistant Professor of Economics at Yale, found inspiration in his economic research on Commitment Contracts. Users log in and follow a four-step process to bring accountability and incentives to bear on a commitment. First, users select their goal. Next, they set the stakes associated with success or failure. The stakes are financial, so they involve funneling money away from the user if a commitment is not carried out. This money can go to a variety of places, including an "anti-charity," or a cause the user vehemently opposes. Third, the user designates a "referee" to ensure there is no fraud. Finally, stickK users can add other stickK users to serve as friendly supporters.

Northwestern Mutual's little green books

Today, all companies have at least some processes to establish goals, track progress, and share commitments. However, Northwestern Mutual Financial Network's green notebooks illustrate accountability principles particularly well. Members of NMFN's sales team carry these small notebooks everywhere they go. After setting sales-related goals, they keep track of their performance inside the green notebook. Within its gridded pages, the notebook captures everything associated with each prospect called. Did he answer the phone? Schedule a meeting? The salespeople refer to their green notebooks as they share their results during weekly reviews with their peers and manager. By doing so, peers are able to share experiences and insights that support each other in their professional development. The practice seems to be working; NMFN has the highest market share and customer loyalty in the industry.

Accountability groups: top ten list

HISTORY IS INTERESTING, BUT you may be so pumped up that you just want quick answers to immediately replicate a full-blown, Dudes-esque structure. The diverse group of twenty-four accountability participants shared their key steps in forming such a group. Ten key actions emerged as requirements in establishing a "heavy" accountability experience. The numbers in parentheses are page numbers, cited to provide immediate access to the parts where you may want more detail.

1. Find two or three fitting partners. Make sure they yearn for accountability, and that you're not just shoving it down their throat. (121)

2. Establish norms for your group covering potential topics such as confidentiality, support, and respect. (139)

3. Establish a regular two-hour block where you can meet every week. Honor this meeting time. (135)

4. Set a general framework or structure for your meetings. (135)

5. Engage each meeting by sharing, critiquing, and empathizing with compassion and a commitment to improving each group member. (131)

6. Choose meaningful goals to become habits that will liberate time, energy, passion, and joy in your life. (83)

7. Lean on your teammates to help you meet these goals and conquer difficult moments. (107)

8. Express your victories and failures to each other. (113)

9. Track your progress on these goals in a way that is readily visible and accessible. (97)

10. When your first goals become habits, come back and set new ones. (83)

Once you make the decisions covered by this list, you are up and running! Of course, each item on the list takes significant time and thought to fine-tune and address in detail. Fortunately, the referenced pages provide that detail.

Or, if you're looking to ease your way into an accountability process, proceed right along to…

The 1st principle: Establishing goals

RALPH WALDO EMERSON AND ANONYMOUS are both attributed as saying, "Sow a thought and you reap an action; sow an act and you reap a habit; sow a habit and you reap a character; sow a character and you reap a destiny." Changing habits leads to changing destinies, and an accountability process can form an ideal backdrop for building powerful habits. The individual goals you set are the fundamental building blocks of the habit-building process. Your partners will boost your goals with an upward prioritization as new habits become integrated into your life.

The Dudes relished pondering which goals they were going to pursue. Conquering each goal provided satisfaction not only because of the thrill of achievement, but also due to the promise and newfound capacity to conquer additional goals. We chose goals that provided rewarding challenges that would maximally enrich our characters. Once you taste the delight of conquering your goals, you will get wrapped up in the thrill of self-mastery. All that life has to offer suddenly seems nearer and more accessible. It's like being a kid in a candy store—except this time you're armed with a twenty.

Like most humans, you probably have an infinite number of goals worth pursuing, but a scarce supply of time, energy, and willpower. You will find that these personal resources grow as you integrate good habits into your life, but you are still ultimately constrained by finite capacity. Given these inescapable constraints, this brief section will serve as an aid to your thought process so you can choose and structure the goals that will make the largest difference.

Approaches to goal selection

CHOOSING YOUR GOALS may be the most exciting part of the whole process. Once you've begun tasting the power of accountability for personal transformation, you may be tempted to use it for every aspiration that you've left on the back burner. You may gleefully entertain notions of finally mastering Swahili and learning to read lips. Don't! This temptation frequently burns people out before they even really get a chance to start. Remember how Jeremy, Connor, and Pete struggled to achieve a flawless performance despite having only a few goals. Many have found that setting the bar too high quickly frustrates them. You don't want to feel like more of a loser than is absolutely necessary!

Avon reinforces the value of starting small, "I found that the biggest risk for me was setting very lofty goals. This has two repercussions associated with it: 1) It can lead to unnecessary frustration. 2) It can lead to false security that a percentage smaller than 100% is good enough."

Connor also recommends going at a reasonable pace, "It's very important to me that my goals be realistic and attainable. It's tempting to make big goals that might be good for me a year down the road, but that doesn't help me now." In this case, setting interim, stepping-stone goals can be a helpful solution.

Choosing the optimal few goals transcends merely capturing stuff that needs to get done. A helpful guiding question can be: Which goals will provide the most joyous, life-transforming impact?

Two to five goals of medium difficulty is often a good starting range. But which two to five goals? There are many excellent books written on the topic of success and goal-setting. In a library, many of them fall under Dewey Decimal number 158.1—my favorite! It corresponds to the subject "Success—psychological aspects." Classics such as *The Seven Habits of Highly Effective People* and other gems from assorted gurus can be found here.

For more immediate gratification, this chapter provides some initial considerations, while the next chapter provides additional thoughts on four broad categories of goals—physical, intellectual, emotional, and spiritual.

Balance

Because accountability rapidly elevates goals to project status, you may do well to choose goals from different categories of life. Choosing all your goals in one category will not provide maximum satisfaction. For example, your goals are to perform a certain number of pushups, sit-ups, laps, and squats every week, it won't feel as though you are taking control of your whole life—just your physical dimension. All sorts of taxonomies exist for divvying up areas of life to ensure balanced pursuit. Take a look at the next chapter to view four broad categories for initial consideration.

Shoulds

Goals fall into this cluster because you have already referred to them numerous times by saying, "I should really ____." You may fill that blank with "go swimming more" or "call that friend" you don't get to see very often. Motivational author and speaker Anthony Robbins notes that we often say we should do so many things—so much so that we "should all over ourselves." It's an odd mystery as to why you don't already do your shoulds. You realize that you enjoy doing them, they lift your spirits, they provide long-term benefits, and you are always glad that you did them afterwards. Yet you rarely do them! Why? Maybe you just forget or you're not in the mood when the moment comes. Turning a should into a real goal combats those two possibilities.

Liberation

Certain activities can have a powerful energizing or coordinating effect that make the rest of your goals easy. These easy actions liberate surprisingly large amounts of time, energy, joy, and motivation. Do these! Just as investors evaluate the ROE—Return On Equity—of their investments, author Brian Tracy speaks of evaluating your personal ROE—Return on Energy. For some, it's spending quality time making sure their to-do daily lists and weekly calendars are tidily established. For others, it's performing a morning exercise or motivational ritual that provides an initial energy that keeps them moving all day.

Self-mastery

Somewhere in your life there's probably a little sloppiness. You may have been trying to hide from it, but it's there. You know it; your friends know it. Maybe you're a little overweight, drink a little too much, have a foul mouth, or keep a cluttered room or messy kitchen. Working on a goal that directly challenges such sloppiness can energize you with a joy and pride in knowing you are successively mastering yourself.

Top-down

What long-term goals do you wish to achieve? What do you want for your relationships, career, finances, spirituality, fitness, contributions to society? Where would you like to be on these dimensions in one year, five years, ten years? The clearer your vision for the long-term goals, the easier it will be to create your weekly goals. For example, if you desire to have a rippling six pack, then you might build in some regular cardiovascular workouts to burn off the belly and abdominal workouts to build the washboard.

The top-down perspective also combats a potentially trou-blesome accountability habit of letting things get out of control. Anne Marie summarizes, "Sometimes it feels as if your goals control your whole life." It's easy to lose sight of why you're doing these things, as the rush of achievement can blind you. Keep the long-term perspective and purpose in mind.

As Jason reminds us, "I try to make my goals less of a to-do list and more of a roadmap to somewhere I want to see myself in the near future. Each week's goals should take me one step closer to that place."

A perfect day

Another handy question is: What would a perfect day look like for you? Think about the activities in which you'd like to effortlessly engage. Such activities are just another name for good habits or virtue. You can paint the scene however you like. Here's an example. You promptly arise alive, alert, and refreshed after seven hours of sleep at 7:00 A.M. You run for two miles, shower, shave, eat a fruity breakfast, and briefly meditate upon the day ahead. You arrive at work earlier than many of your coworkers and clear your inbox, bringing the number of emails down to zero…

Blasts of inspiration

After you think about anything long and hard, new ideas will probably strike you at odd times—such as when you're in the shower or when you're about to fall asleep. Be sure to capture them with a notepad before they disappear. I'm personally a huge fan of the Moleskine pocket cahiers, notecard shoved in the wallet, or iPhone for on-the-go goal capture.

A little help from your friends

The Dudes started by having everyone brainstorm goal ideas for one another. Such an approach will probably be highly beneficial for your group if you already know each other well. Or, you can simply brainstorm your own goals with the group to get inspiration from them and vice versa. Morgan shares how her group set their goals, "During our first meeting we just wrote every single thing we wanted to work on. Then we chose the ones that would be the essential building blocks and the easiest ones to start with."

Favorite goals in four categories

HOWEVER YOU CHOOSE YOUR GOALS, make sure that your goals are important to you and that you truly desire some helpful peer pressure to make them happen. Suddenly, these items become a priority in your life because you have people consistently prodding you to perform them. The prodding makes the experience like that of the "boss-man." So make sure to pick things worth prodding!

Below are a few examples in bullet point across four broad categories: physical, emotional, intellectual, and spiritual. These lists may provide initial inspiration or highlight a blind spot in your life. The paragraphs elaborate further on recurring accountability favorites.

Note that all of these goals are trackable actions with an illustrative number associated with them. You clearly know if you hit them or you missed them. Being able to measure success is absolutely key for the next section, "Tracking performance."

Physical goals

- Three cardiovascular sessions of at least thirty minutes a week
- Two weight training sessions—including twelve total sets—a week
- No days will contain more than four alcoholic beverages consumed
- Be completely out of bed prior to 7:15 A.M. every day
- Don't ever touch the snooze button
- Sleep at least seven hours every night
- Take a vitamin or recommended medicine everyday at a certain time
- Drink sixty ounces of water every day
- Floss every day

"I don't have time" is favorite excuse to avoid exercise; however, you could also think of exercise as a means of creating time. The time invested in exercise yields additional energy to catch up on the work you weren't doing while you were exercising. Energy is released immediately following the workout, your metabolism is elevated throughout the day, and you sleep better. Finally, exercisers live longer and have more years on this earth to do what they put off while exercising!

Accountability people who commit to exercise tend to have best results when they try doing a variety of different bodily challenges—rather than falling in love with only one. To over-generalize, men may relish the bench press and arm exercises, neglecting legs or cardio. Meanwhile, women might focus solely on cardio. But performing unappealing exercises enhances self-discipline all the more. Additionally, when challenged in multiple ways, the body stretches more to adapt. You can learn from your accountability partners' different styles of exercise—and having a built-in spotter at the gym is pretty handy.

Hydration can also make a powerful impact on vitality levels, but it is very easy to forget. As such, it makes a great addition to your goal repertoire. Try setting a realistic level of water consumption. Maybe eight eight-ounce glasses a day or four giant cups. Just set up a system that works for you. Whenever you're feeling thirsty, that means that your body is crying out to you that it has urgent need of water. Hydrating before you are thirsty helps prevent the daytime slowdowns. Don't just re-hydrate, pre-hydrate!

Others fail to get enough sleep. Forfeiting sleep in this nation seems to be portrayed as some sort of heroic virtue. The mythology is that hard-working people of impact have too many obligations to get a decent night's sleep. False! For many people, the highlight of their day is going to sleep. This always struck me as unfortunate. Should the best part of the day really occur while unconscious?! Figuring out how much sleep you need and making it a priority can really change your life outlook. Try getting ample sleep for a few nights to recognize precisely how much of a difference adequate sleep makes in your daily experience of aliveness. You may discover that it's worth slimming down your evening schedule to get to bed on time and be fully alive during the daytime. Plus, it's a blast to score points for sleeping! Being obligated to sleep feels gleefully refreshing.

Emotional goals

- Call the parents, kids, or other relation at least once a week
- Spend two hours with a close friend you don't see very often
- Spend ten minutes tidying your living or work space every day
- Track every dollar you spend
- Reply to all voicemails and emails within thirty-six hours
- Sincerely tell your spouse you love him / her at least once every day

A favorite emotional goal for most is spending time with a priority human that's being neglected. Having one or two hours with that forgotten friend can lift your whole emotional health. Try constructing a list of the people you love, so you can refer to it and say, "Hey, I haven't talked to him in two months!" then make the call.

Kathleen touches upon the under-rated power of emotional goals, "In the stress that is my life, I often push friends and family to the back burner and view them as a luxury that I can only afford when all of my other work is done. Yet I know from experience that all of that other work only continues to build up and is never really done... after a few weeks of regularly meeting with friends, I was de-stressed and riding on cloud nine."

Intellectual goals

- Spend twenty minutes a day reading a book for pleasure or personal development
- Spend eight hours a week studying for a significant test (e.g. GRE, GMAT, LSAT, MCAT, CPA) or class
- Every evening, take some time to plan out the next day
- Review life mission and long-term goals every morning
- Identify the five most important things to be accomplished at the beginning of each day
- Complete every item designated as "crucial" on the daily to-do list

Planning is a theme running across favorite goals in the intellectual domain. Planning is a powerful act of will that takes control of your life away from circumstances and returns it to your hands. Some form of structure—be it a checklist, calendar, spreadsheet, or list of goals often goes a long way. Speaker Zig Ziglar loves pointing out that you can't hit a target that isn't there.

Spiritual goals

- Examine your life, actions, and impact for six minutes every night
- Pray for twenty minutes every day
- Spend fifteen minutes in reflection / journal writing every day
- Spent four minutes in complete silence every morning
- Give up a meal once a week
- Visit a temple / mosque / church / house of worship every week
- Give 10% of your income to worthy organizations
- Spend two hours volunteering each week
- Snap a rubber band on your wrist every time you have a hateful, selfish, addictive, or other thought you deem inappropriate

The spiritual life is easily neglected, so it's intuitive that accountability partners frequently report significant spiritual gains. Consistent, daily dedication to the spiritual life can yield powerful results. Many believe in God, but relatively few spend consistent daily time in prayer. Accountability partners have discovered that committing to something small but daily can spark remarkable transformation. Ten minutes of prayer or stillness is a great way to kick-start the spiritual life. People become surprised and delighted by the peaceful and/or supernatural wonder in their lives when they finally stop to pay attention.

The 2nd principle: Tracking performance

YOU LOVE IT. YOUR BOSS LOVES IT. Everyone wants to increase it. You look for it in your investments and sports cars. Performance. Results. The bottom line. The proof is in the pudding. Something inside each of us is skeptical of any venture—no matter how much fun it may be—that doesn't provide the results. Meanwhile, another piece of us just loves accumulating points. Credit card points, airline miles, high scores…points wield power. P.J. sums it up nicely when he says, "I crave points like I crave White Castle."

Chris also feels the urge, "Every time I look at my spreadsheet I always want more points. I want more success."

The Dudes obsessed over the elusive 100% score. There was something glorious about attaining The Perfect Result. However, a 100% would not exist if they weren't keeping track. You can't win if you're not keeping score! If our goals persisted as vague intentions, like they did during the first meeting, then flawless victories could not be fully appreciated or celebrated. Were we really 100% complete? Without tracking, there is no way to say authoritatively that you are fully victorious. How successful were you? Pretty successful? Very successful? Having some means of recording your performance is essential to knowing how well you're doing and seeing how far you've come. Noting a jump from 40 out of 50 actions accomplished to 48 out of 50 is significant—and a source of pride. Granted, some things are not quantifiable, but experience has shown that you can always find a proxy!

You may be tempted to "wing it" and not keep a clear record of your performance. Don't! This sidesteps the positive pain that hard numbers provide. It also precludes the pride of seeing your improvement. If you're stumped, this section will provide a variety of potential tracking solutions. From the simplicity of a checklist to the sophisticated data analysis capacities of a spreadsheet, you'll discover a way to record your victories and relish your ascent. It also provides reward and punishment mechanisms to further enhance the power of keeping score.

Assorted tracking techniques

Ben Franklin's matrix

ONE OF THE FIRST AMERICANS pioneering the progress of virtue was Benjamin Franklin. This audacious man started with a list of thirteen virtues. He would tackle one virtue a week and make a mark every day he felt he had committed a violation against such a virtue. Quoted from his autobiography (complete with old spellings), are his definitions for virtues, and how he accounted for them each week.

Franklin reports:

"I made a little book, in which I allotted a page for each of the virtues…I might mark, by a little black spot, every fault I found upon examination to have been committed respecting that virtue upon that day."

Virtue	S	M	T	W	R	F	S
TEMPERANCE. Eat not to dullness; drink not to elevation.					●		
SILENCE. Speak not but what may benefit others or yourself; avoid trifling conversation.							
ORDER. Let all your things have their places; let each part of your business have its time.							
RESOLUTION. Resolve to perform what you ought; perform without fail what you resolve.							
FRUGALITY. Make no expense but to do good to others or yourself; i.e. waste nothing.							
INDUSTRY. Lose no time; be always employ'd in something useful; cut off all unnecessary actions.							
SINCERITY. Use no hurtful deceit; think innocently and justly, and, if you speak, speak accordingly.							
JUSTICE. Wrong none by doing injuries, or omitting the benefits that are your duty.							
MODERATION. Avoid extremes; forbear resenting injuries so much as you think they deserve.							
CLEANLINESS. Tolerate no uncleanliness in body, cloaths, or habitation.							
TRANQUILLITY. Be not distubed at trifles, or at accidents common or unavoidable.							
CHASTITY. Rarely use venery but for health or offspring, never to dullness, weakness, or the injury of your own or another's peace or reputation.							
HUMILITY. Imitate Jesus and Socrates.							

This chart demonstrates what would have happened if Ben couldn't resist the "Thirsty Thursdays" special at the nearby tavern. However, you might be well advised to be a bit more specific about your goals. You may be more lenient with yourself than Mr. Franklin as to what constitutes a failure unless you have clearly defined what success and failure look like.

Wall charts

Some accountable folks enjoy regressing to the good old days of their childhood, where gold stars were the currency du jour. One group set up a chart with each member of the accountability group on the rows and the weeks on the columns. If any given member delivers a 100% performance in one of four performance areas (physical, intellectual, emotional, spiritual), she gets a star. Each of the performance areas has a different color, so a perfect week would result in four different-colored stars filling up the column for that week.

Or, each day can be evaluated on a star system, so you pause at the end of each day to reflect and recall if you earned one—and do some last minute work! Similarly, Samantha makes "a chart on printer or construction paper. It is just a simple grid, but then I use stickers… I tape mine to my desk so that I always see it and remember what I need to get done."

I've also seen large posted charts being used at the workplace. A group of co-workers sitting in the vicinity vows to support each other in regular exercise. Workers will record their efforts on a giant post-it note in a matrix, with days being the rows and people being the columns. If there's a lot of white space in a column, the co-workers can provide a correction!

Lists and journals

For some, nothing tops an old-fashioned checkmark on the to-do list. Jenny reports, "I tally a goal every time I do it once. Then I get a checkmark when the entire goal is completed. I love check marks. If I could marry my check marks, I probably would." List users generally share the blank list with their accountability members at the meetings and then report on their performance against that list at the next meeting. These lists can be tucked nicely into a journal / planner / calendar that records other life happenings. Or you can have a calendar strictly for accountability goals to help you allocate the appropriate amount of time. Then the key contents of that week's journal entries can be shared at the meetings.

Websites

A host of websites, including www.stickk.com and www.43things.com, offer high-tech approaches to goal-tracking. Since much of the power of these sites comes from their abilities to publicize your commitments, you will learn more about these when you read the third principle, "Sharing commitments."

For office dwellers, websites highlight a theme running through all the systems: constant visibility. Benjamin Franklin carried the little notebook charting his virtue progress with him wherever he went. The chart users keep them present wherever they go. To-do list makers have them on their desk. Spreadsheet users (coming up next) have the file constantly open in their computers. Laura says, "I need that constant reminder, something screaming at me: 'You want to be excellent! You need to do this every day and make it an integral part of your life. You need to make it a habit!'"

The spreadsheet

I personally find the spreadsheet to be the most rigorous and flexible tracking system, but my preference doesn't make it the best for you and your group. The spreadsheet provides several key advantages, such as automatically calculated percentages so that you can easily compare your progress to previous weeks. It provides a digitized and automated sort of "report card" for how a week went. Rob likes the worksheets because they give the group "a serious, business approach to our work."

Spreadsheets might elicit a visceral unpleasant reaction—"Spreadsheets, the things of business or hardcore competitive types—yuck!" It need not be so. While still a student, Kathleen reported, "It makes

my goals more tangible to see them expressed as points and percentages. It's real motivation to see how much I can boost my success
rate by doing the things listed in my spreadsheet."

Many find quantifying a week's performance in such a fashion especially enlivening and empowering. Avon describes
how "after achieving my first round of progress, I couldn't wait
to get back to my place to move those numbers up. I found
myself running to get back to my computer to put it in." Others liken it to converting life into a fast-paced, high-scoring
video game.

Here's a picture of what a simple spreadsheet might look
like:

Goals	Swearing	Prayer	Exercise	Sleep	Reading
Total Occurrences Desired	7	21	6	7	7
Current Score	0%	0%	0%	0%	0%
Feb. 6					
Feb. 7					
Feb. 8					
Feb. 9					
Feb. 10					
Feb. 11					
Feb. 12					
		Overall	0.0%		

The bricks-and-mortar of the spreadsheet is the grid. In
this example, the columns are the goals and the rows are the
days. Each cell within the grid is an intersection between goal
and day. Thus, each cell provides a place for you to report
what you did with a goal on a particular day. The overall performance for each goal is the fraction of the goal completed

over the amount of goal desired. For example, if the goal was to study for five hours, but you studied for four hours, then the percentage performance would be eighty percent. The overall week's performance is generated by averaging the performance of the other goals. So, if you score eighty percent on two goals and one-hundred percent on two other goals, then you'd earn an averaged overall score of ninety percent for the week. Technical instructions for creating your own worksheets can be found in the appendix. Or, you can just use the tools available on www.teamupbook.com to get a leg-up on the process.

As discussed in the goal-setting section, goals will ideally take the form of specific actions that can be objectively distinguished as complete or incomplete at the end of a week. Several techniques for quantifying follow, but the key to all of them is being as specific as possible.

Binary

This system is probably the easiest—even the first computers understood it. You start by deciding what defines an "occurrence." Try making your definition explicit, so there's less room for cheating. For example, you can make "exercise" mean no less than thirty minutes of cardiovascular activity and 8 sets of weight training. Or you can have "reflection" mean no less than twenty minutes of meditation with at least a page of journaling. Again, write it down and share it with your group because—if you're like me—you'll be tempted to cheat later.

After having defined an occurrence, each cell can receive either a 1 or a 0 based on whether or not that occurrence happened. Did you do exercise on Monday? Put a 1 in the Exercise/Monday intersection. Did you fail to reflect on Tuesday? Put a 0 in that cell.

Output

Many goals have a number conveniently built into them. You may desire to perform three hundred pushups, mail one hundred letters, or make forty cold calls. Such goals are often quite motivating because you feel like you're racking up big numbers and can see progress with the smallest amount of effort. This one is really good for writing or tasks that can feel repetitive. One of my goals was to draft one thousand words of this book each week, and it felt great to see big numbers appear!

Time

You may find it convenient to express your goal in terms of time units. You could declare that you're going to spend eight hours studying or two hundred minutes conversing with distant friends over the course of your week. Be careful of measuring time spent in some ventures. If you're easily tempted to cheat, using time as a measurement allows you to score your points even if you perform your actions (e.g. exercise) in a distracted, lackluster manner.

Creative solutions

You may note that some things are difficult to quantify. Ask your partners for suggestions and consider trying what these accountability folks have used as solutions:

- Liz says, "When someone has a goal that is harder to quantify, they must tell the story of how they accomplished that goal."
- Jill says, "Every time that someone does X they must also do Y. If they don't, then they get a zero."
- Rob says, "Stuff that's too hard to quantify is just set as a limit or a range. For example . . . I have a limit of four drinks or less per outing."

Rewards and punishments

TRACKING MAKES REWARDS AND PUNISHMENTS all the more possible. Striving for excellence with the help of your friends provides for plenty of intrinsic joy. However, adding rewards and punishments into the mix makes the joys and sorrows associated with performance all the more tangible. For example, delivering eighty pushups to make amends has a powerful way of communicating to yourself that you don't want to do that again!

In selecting your rewards and punishments, choose a level of intensity that suits all the members of your group. Everyone is different in terms of personal sensitivity and what motivates them. Some people are naturally hard on themselves; being scorned can be more hurtful than helpful. And some punishments just don't do it for everyone. For example, pushups won't do the trick to punish the one who relishes pummeling his pectorals. Touch base periodically to see if you are providing the right incentives.

Some recommendations follow. Note that many of the punishments may rely on a particularly quantitative tracking methodology. You can alter them to mesh with the particular tracking process you select.

Rewards

- **Verbal kudos.** Meaningful compliments are simple, natural, and free. These should flow frequently and naturally— accountability is hard work!
- **Food and beverage.** Everyone may consume some special treats for each group member who has performed at the predetermined level. Toasts, cheers, whooping, and hollering are in order.

- **The slow clap.** Breakthrough performances deserve breakthrough recognition. When a member performs something noteworthy, the other members can "spontaneously" break into the slow clap. This dramatic device sometimes occurs at the end of movies. It occurs when one person begins slowly clapping, as others gradually join in and increase volume, gradually accelerating until the applause is loud and hearty. I can attest that people feel wonderfully appreciated when receiving such adulation.

- **The main event.** When everyone gets a 100% or other pre-determined high level of performance, the whole group goes out for celebration. Fancy restaurant, Mini-golf, movie, bars, dessert, you name it. Lindsay, Sam, and Morgan opted to have a Mary Kay party when they all got a 100%.

- **The victory dance.** Is there a glorious power song you'd like to hear when you achieve victory? Perhaps some funky moves you've been saving for a special occasion. Some say emotion is created by motion, so cut loose... you've earned it!

Punishments

- **Physical challenge.** Punishing the body sends strong messages to the brain. Pushups are a favorite way to make this happen. For example, you can agree to perform one pushup for each 1/10th of a percent below 100%. So, a 90% would mean one hundred pushups. Other options include laps, crunches, sprints, or repetitions of any exercise of your choice. For added dramatic effect, you can have each person do them during your gatherings while the other partners are barking out the counts. Connor, Rich, Chris, and Dan sometimes hit the person performing his physical challenge with pillows or other innocuous objects. Others incorporate pump up music ("The Eye of the Tiger" is a perennial favorite) into the physical challenges.

- **Cash money.** Fine members an amount of money based on each percentage they fall below a perfect score. Depending on the size of your bankroll, this could be a nickel, dime, quarter, dollar, or $100 bill. Whatever's meaningful and appropriate for all. So, at the quarter-a-point level, earning a 96% means you'd contribute $1.

- **Self-denial.** Determine a particular level of performance that qualifies as completely unacceptable. Communicate that threshold with the group. If anyone's performance drops below the threshold, the low-performer must forego something he enjoys (e.g. dessert or TV).

- **Harsh words.** Assuming everyone has agreed in advance that they can handle it, some prickly verbiage can provide some real motivation. Just imagining the dread of hearing a "You sicken me" can be adequate to conquer the real-time temptation to slack.

- **Dares.** The person who receives the lowest score for the week has to perform a dare determined by the other members in the group. Maybe wear a shirt of shame or do something totally wacky. Hilarity ensues.

So, you have unlimited options when designing rewards and punishments. Try structuring your rewards and punishments along several dimensions. Combining different methods can boost the effectiveness.

Try mixing and matching categories of:	Which can be assigned to:
• Pleasant things	• Each measure short of perfection
• Unpleasant things	• The perfect performing individual
• Individual incentives	• Meeting pre-established benchmarks
	• High performer rewards
• Group-based incentives	• Low performer punishments

Tactics for increasing your score

INEVITABLY, ONCE YOU BEGIN TRACKING—and rewarding—your performance, you will want to see the numbers go up. The following tips can boost your score.

Calling your shot

Although it may seem expected that people will perform as best they can every week, there is something powerful in declaring, "Next week, I shall deliver a flawless performance." Just saying the words aloud makes the difference. It enhances the power of accountability against future temptations, as your mind is likely to say, "Well, I promised a perfect score. I need to get it done."

Visualization

Crisply, clearly, and powerfully envision what you will be doing with your week. Imagine the elation of victory and the sensations that will accompany that. It is especially helpful to engage in morning visualization for what you will do during the day, or as you plan the following day. Picturing the result increases your motivation.

Pacing

Plan out the week in advance. Recognize where you will be busy and where you won't. Make sure to allocate time for rest, relaxation, and fun. If your week has some extra obligations, reduce your commitment to accountability goals. Make sure that you are engaged in a challenging yet uplifting workload. Don't kill yourself or be unrealistic. If you have a friend coming into town for a few days, figure out how to get him involved (e.g., running together), or adjust your goals for that particular week accordingly, rather than always repeating the prior week's load.

Check-ins

Talk to your accountability partners frequently—not just at your meetings! Often they provide the reminder and push necessary to get you through a difficult or tiring day. Additionally, many accountable people have said that they bond the most when they engage in activities outside the "formal" environment of a meeting. Some partnerships operate by having a short call every morning.

Dailies

It's often easier to build a daily habit than it is to do something two or three times a week. Daily habits are especially manageable if you can link the action to a particular time of day—such as just after you wake up, after your shower immediately, after lunch, or shortly before bed time. Psychologists say it takes twenty-one consecutive days to build a daily habit. It seems to take more occurrences to build a habit that isn't occurring daily.

Scheduling

Allocating the time necessary to accomplish tasks goes a long way to actually accomplishing the tasks. Block out some time for yourself in your planner or Outlook calendar. Also, people find that the more they strive to keep their commitments to accountability partners, the better they are at keeping commitments to themselves.

Momentum

Right after an accountability meeting, attack some goals! Tap into that healthy rush to get ahead of the week. Then, you may feel an extra ounce of motivation to keep from "throwing away" that head start.

The 3rd principle: Sharing commitments

SPEAKING YOUR COMMITMENTS ALOUD is the final piece to making them real. This sharing also tremendously enriches relationships. Just imagine what a weekly sharing of your most intimate dreams, hopes, goals, desires, frustrations, victories, and failures can do for your relationships.

In Aristotle's *Ethics*, he identifies three categories of friends: friends of pleasure, friends of utility, and true friends. Friends of pleasure may gratify through their hilarity or access to particularly cool entertainment. Friends of utility provide value by being useful—such as business acquaintances or dispensers of wisdom. True friends, however, provide for lasting happiness by supporting each other in the pursuit of virtue. That is, they support you in your quest to build solid habits that result in the good life. Sound familiar?

We didn't realize it at the time, but the members in our group were growing into the true friendships that Aristotle describes. At each of our meetings, we demanded excellence of one another, pushing each other towards virtue. To Aristotle, it would be no surprise that our relationships were so enriched! Kathleen explains: "It's so awesome to have friends who love you too much to let you remain as you are." Would you like to take a few acquaintances and move into true friendship with them? This section will provide some ways to do just that.

And even if you're not ready to dive directly into this kind of intimacy, this section highlights how to begin sharing your commitments and building those relationships. Should you choose to dig deeper, you'll learn the finer points of choosing the members of your group as well as how to establish the rules and structure of your interactions.

Commitment sharing — light

Up until now, most of these techniques and approaches have been implementable whether you're pursuing a "light" or "heavy" model of accountability. However, most of the content in this section discusses how to find committed partners and provides thoughts for optimally engaging in sensitive conversations. If for whatever reason, you're not ready to bring your friends into all this, don't shy away from commitment sharing altogether. Some options exist for you to ease into things.

Friendly wagers

You don't have to bare your entire soul to enjoy a little pressure to achieve specific goals. It can be as easy as establishing a weekly email cadence with a friend. If you have the same goal, you can make it competitive (e.g. whoever runs the most miles in a week owes the other $20). Or, you could have completely independent goals and just mark your points if you achieve your goals.

Hire somebody

Numerous professions are more than happy to take your money in exchange for the accountability that comes built into their other services. Indeed, much of the value of a personal trainer comes from you parting with money in exchange for work-out appointments. Skipping a work out can mean you're out of cash and in for a lecture.

Beyond the physical realm, coaches exist for any function imaginable. For example, the executive coaching and life coaching industries are growing at a rapid clip. Despite its silly portrayal in some sitcoms, life coaching really is maturing as a discipline and profession. There's no shame in hiring one.

Therapists and mental health professionals also have accountability elements built into their sessions. Quality health insurance plans, combined with a diminished taboo associated with seeing therapists, make these professionals more accessible than you might imagine. Finally, I'd personally be more than happy to kick your butt—for a nominal charge!

Make an appointment

You can add accountability into any goal by inviting someone else to join in at a specific time and place. Want to exercise in the mornings? Schedule a recurring appointment with a buddy who works out at your gym. Want to hunker down and plow through that Russian novel? Establish a reading date at a café or library. You can enhance this tactic if you entrust your partner with vital materials and vice versa. You might try swapping gym bags, running shoes, wallets, or cell phones to build the pressure.

Pre-existing groups

Community organizations offer many ready-made options to incorporate light accountability. Paying dues and becoming an official member begins to create group expectations and a little pull that begins influencing you. You don't want to be that guy who never shows up! If you're looking to plug into your community, you can join the Rotary, Lions, Kiwanis, or a nonprofit board. If you want to improve your public speaking, check out Toastmasters. If you want to synch up with like-minded professionals, attend chamber of commerce meetings or networking groups. The list goes on and on.

Online resources

The Internet makes it easier than ever to broadcast commitments and performance. For example, some Weight Watchers participants post videos of their weigh-ins on YouTube. You could commit to post your performance on particular goals publicly via a status update on Facebook or a tweet on Twitter. Imagine telling your entire online follower base, "Ran zero times this week out of a committed four." That could increase your motivation in a hurry! And while you're tweeting, don't be shy about messaging @optimal_pete or dropping the #teamup hashtag. I'd love to hear from you.

If you really want to intensify the broadcast, try ShoutNow, at www.shoutnow.com. ShoutNow calls all the phone numbers you provide to play a voice message you pre-record from your phone. You might enlist a corps of ten people who care to receive phone updates that say, "Hello, this is Pete with a pre-recorded message informing you that I've achieved all my week's objectives."

Other web resources are specifically dedicated to accountability purposes. You've read about stickK in the "Brief history of accountability" chapter. Others abound! While it can be worthwhile to shop around a bit, these sites are fairly similar to each other, so you may just want to stick with the one that grabs you first, rather than trying to learn many systems.

- **www.43things.com** enlists users to make a list of things they want to achieve within their lifetime, share progress, and cheer others onward to victory.
- **www.comotivate.com** matches users with "buddies" based on similar goals and other criteria. Users form teams with these buddies.
- **www.goalforit.com** offers goal-setting and tracking software and also boasts of its capability to create "chore charts kids will love."
- **www.goalmigo.com** allows you to post goals and invite others to support you.

- **www.goaltribe.com** facilitates setting action plans and identifying allies who see your score to help you improve over time.
- **www.joesgoals.com** offers a simple grid interface to facilitate tracking of daily goals each week.
- **www.mecanbe.com** also allows users to establish goals and identify the tasks required to reach them, forming robust plans.

Other sites lend support to specific goal areas:

- **www.mint.com** awards points based on which steps you take toward your financial fitness.
- **www.nike.com** offers goal setting, tracking, and sharing for running distances and programs. The system can also plug-in with technology for certain Apple devices that measures distance.
- **www.peertrainer.com** facilitates sharing fitness goals with groups.
- **www.revolutionhealth.com** integrates personal health records with online health tools and trackers.
- **www.myfooddiary.com**, **www.sparkpeople.com**, and **www.thedailyplate.com** track your nutrition and exercise history. Users can estimate calories consumed and burned in order to predict weight loss.

Choosing your party

WHO WILL BE MY PARTNERS? This question is of paramount importance, and it deserves great consideration. Even if a group of people just leaps to mind, take a step back to carefully consider. If you're just looking for a little extra friendly pressure, many folks will do. If, however, you're looking to engage in more personal exchanges, this chapter will provide useful initial considerations.

First, determine the number of people you want in your group. The optimal number depends primarily upon the structure of your meetings and time available. If you want your conversations to run both deeply and broadly within a one- or two-hour weekly meeting, you will be limited to two or three partners. Several practical considerations limit the number of people, but the biggest considerations are scheduling and meeting length.

Simply put, it's hard to get everyone together. It becomes increasingly difficult to find meeting times that everyone can attend as you increase the number of your members. In a deep-sharing world, attendance of every member is vital. The point of such a group's existence is to foster a sense of accountability and infuse support into everyone's week. A group quickly learns that a missing person is felt by the whole group; it hurts and makes everything feel incomplete. Indeed, a well-functioning group will only meet when all parties are in place—even if this means deviating from its scheduled time.

Additionally, a meeting's length increases dramatically with each additional member you add. If everyone is commenting on everyone else, then your total number of conversations increases exponentially with each additional person. For example, if you have three people, each person will share his story, then the two others comment on it. These three conversations will repeat for each participant, for a total of nine conversations. The chart illustrates:

People	Conversations
2	4
3	9
4	16
5	25
6	36

Because the number of conversations is the square of the number of people, a meeting with four people often takes nearly twice as long as a meeting with three people. Having six people sharing in such a format would force the meeting to take a huge chunk of time or require a reduction in depth of sharing.

Next question: Who? If you already have a group of two or three friends who are close, motivated, and open with each other, then inserting some accountability into the mix is a natural and beautiful way to take your friendships to the next level. Most groups formed this way; someone had people in mind, heard about accountability, shared it with them, and away they went! Other times the process can feel more iterative. You try it with a group of four, then there's a troublesome party who drops out. You do it with three for a while, then another person hears about your amazing results and wants in. The cycle continues.

However, if you don't have a pre-existing crew that leaps to mind, then you have the challenge of assembling the ideal team. Accountability practitioners have taken several different approaches to this. Sometimes you can just feel it in your gut, as Buddy explains, "I chose close friends who I knew I'd be able to share my deepest secrets and those who cared about my well being." That will do it.

Others require more meditation upon the question of optimal teammates. Indeed, just planting the question in your mind can be fruitful. If the question is in the back of your head, you will begin subtly evaluating the people in your daily interactions. As you bump into your daily acquaintances, ask yourself if that person would make a good accountability partner? Such questions can help you locate your crew without much difficulty.

If you still aren't quite sure, take heart. In my research on accountability groups, more people commented on what makes an ideal accountability partner than on any other topic. As such, principles and questions for identifying optimal accountability partners form the whole next chapter.

The ideal accountability partner

WITH GOOD REASON, people love their accountability partners—and love talking about them! This section captures their thoughts on what makes an accountability partner so great for the job. As you read through wonderful qualities in accountability partners, it may help to have an initial list of humans in the back of your mind. Here are a few questions to help you generate such a list:

- Whom do I admire?
- With whom would I like to grow closer?
- Who shares my deepest values?
- Whom do I really trust?
- Who seems highly motivated?
- Who really seems to be striving for excellence?
- Who could really commit to and get excited about this process?
- Who seems able to give and receive honest feedback without being too offended?
- Who has expressed frustration at falling short of their expectations or initiatives?

Armed with such a questionnaire, think about your people—friends, family, coworkers, everyone! Ask yourself how well they may measure up against the following four themes. You can think of them as the four C's—comfort, courage, commitment, and compassion.

Comfort

Underpinning the whole process, you'll want accountability partners who you feel comfortable telling everything. Really everything. Matt says, "Having a partner that you can be open with is probably the most key trait…If honesty cannot be involved, goals get set for mostly superficial items instead of real life-changing habits." Ideally, your interactions will have a fun, comfortable vibe. This comfort enables you to really let loose about your frustrations, addictions, aspirations, peculiarities, fantasies, joys, and vices. Sharing your vulnerabilities is much of what cements the accountability bond.

Comfort seems to depend on two things: trust and personal dynamics. Avon emphasizes, "If the group members cannot trust each other, the group will either fall apart or each meeting will be a waste of time. Mutual trust and camaraderie must be built first before accountability can flourish." The preeminence of trust explains why most accountability groups form from existing sets of good friends.

While trust is the predominant factor of comfort, other personal dynamic issues matter as well. Ideally, you will share certain values, be it faith, career, fitness, or entrepreneurship. If someone doesn't respect your precious goals, it will quickly kill the comfort vibe. Anne Marie provides several final factors to consider on comfort, "Make sure you and your group members have complementary personalities, enjoy being together, and respect each other." Also be on guard for jealousy or competitiveness. You may want to avoid people with whom you compete for promotions, grades, or business. If you feel uneasy about a potential accountability partner, address it or exit! Even if you think someone's just plain weird—and not in a charming way—you will either need to tackle that issue or find a new group.

Courage

Even in the presence of big comfort, you still might hesitate to share that extremely personal part of yourself. Hence, the need for courage. No matter how cozy you feel with your accountability partners, there will be some yucky things about you that you just don't want to say—especially to these people for whom you hold such admiration. You and your partners will need to summon personal courage to tackle that stuff. Kelly pinpoints the difficulty, "It is really hard to admit some of the things I struggle with to my group members. They are all amazing women and sometimes I fear them thinking less of me."

Courage in accountability is two-pronged, however. It requires courage to share yourself and perhaps even more courage to point out faults in an accountability partner. Jeremy points out this criterion may well quickly dwindle your list: "Very few of us have friends that will give it to us straight… you need the type of friends who 'just might' be able to give it to you straight."

Samantha echoes Jeremy's point: "You need someone who won't be afraid to show his or her disappointment in you. If your partner always lets your mistakes slide, neither of you are going to get very far." When three people are equipped with the boldness to openly share and fully critique, you have a powerful posse!

Commitment

The accountability process provides an excellent return on investment, but demands a substantial personal commitment to work well. Rich tells the blunt truth, "If you don't really want to improve, don't join. It won't always be easy and glorious. It takes hard work to break habits or form new ones." Ideal accountability partners tend to have a passion for realizing their full potential. Such a passion may reveal itself in the faithful practice of an art, excellence in athletics, or a penchant for the self-improvement section of book stores.

Conversely, it's maddening trying to ignite the fire underneath someone who just doesn't have it. They have to want it badly and want it for themselves. Avon reports, "Accountability cannot be shoved down everyone's throat. It works for those who are open to recognize shortcomings in their lives." Groups who have dealt with the issue report that not only does the non-committed party miss out on the power of mutual accountability, but their lackluster attitude also stalls the overall group's momentum. Flaky persons will either need to address their fickleness or go elsewhere.

Compassion

At the same time, Mr. or Ms. Hard Core Accountability can be a bit off-putting. Greg notes, "The ideal partner is someone who realizes that this stuff is hard. Changing behaviors is often very difficult, especially for people who love to procrastinate."

Laura summarizes by noting the ideal accountability partner "is full of love…will push you to become a better person, but support you in times of failure." Genuinely caring about each others' well-being is essential to enable the sharing and feedback that uplifts—rather than destroys—a person.

The four C's provide a handy framework to identify an ideal accountability partner, but don't forget to take into account some practical considerations:

- **Proximity**. If some of your people live on the other side of the continent, then you will not be able to gather everyone regularly. Email, webcams, and telephone may get the job done after you've already developed the accountability bond, but for starting a group, they don't quite do the trick. The group experience often includes shouts of celebration, hugging, and other factors that technology just cannot replicate—especially if you aren't already close.

- **Gender**. Men and women are simply different. As such, complete relating, sharing, and understanding may occur best within groups that are all male or all female. Spouses represent one notable exception; if you're married, you hopefully already have a bond stronger than the accountability bond. See the chapter "Gender and accountability" for more thoughts on this.

- **Faith**. In the story of The Dudes, the Catholic faith was a strong, shared commitment among the men and framed our worldview as we were working together. It is helpful for partners to share values on core issues. See the chapter "On faith" for more thoughts on this matter.

After you've narrowed your list to a few special people, try to find a single ally completely onboard with you. That person will be the one who responds extremely enthusiastically. Maybe this person has other ideal friends in mind. Then, set up some informal gatherings with the two of you and at least one other candidate. Introduce your ally to these people and vice versa to see who clicks best. Personality can be a mysterious factor. It's odd how you can get along well with two different people, but those two don't share any sort of connection.

When reflecting all these questions and the four C's, Connor suggests what could well be a fifth C: Caution. He warns that a common mistake is "choosing people who you think should be in accountability instead of people who actually want to be in accountability really badly. You're dealing with people, so you can't just invest time and energy and expect them to change. They have to will it themselves, so the search for partners requires conversation, not reflection."

Thinking about accountability partners can only get you to the candidate stage. Ultimately, the real fireworks occur when your partners make the choice. And when they do, the sight is spectacular.

On faith

THE ROLE OF FAITH is a bedrock component of many accountability groups—so much so that it deserves explicit attention. Accountability groups have a rich history in the Christian tradition. The Dudes' faith brought us together powerfully and provided an all-encompassing context to our accountability endeavors. Underlying all our goals was a desire to grow in virtue and imitate Jesus Christ.

Many of the accountability groups I surveyed had a significant faith component, so I asked these faithful: "Do you think this can work without religion?" The answer was a resounding yes. The positive pressures that stem from the power of a promise, the desire to avoid looking bad, and the motivation to keep your word assist in building habits. You've read about the positive effects from Master Mind and other groups that had no emphasis on spirituality.

That said, as a person of faith, I believe that God supernaturally turbocharges the whole process. The presence of a spiritual mission can enhance everything, charging it with a special aliveness. Kelly says, "It helps a lot knowing that all of our main goals in life are to become holy. We know that when our group members are calling us on something it is because they want to help us get to Heaven—not just point out our faults."

Additionally, because faith is such an intimate part of a person, sharing it regularly can really draw people together. However, sharing other high-level values with your accountability partners will also provide a special charge. Maybe you share the fiery ambition of entrepreneurship or a strong commitment to family first. Those too can tightly bind a group. Disagreements are fine, but if a key difference in values reduces an accountability partner's respect for another's goals—be it faith-oriented or otherwise—group performance dwindles.

Whatever your current position on faith, bear in mind that growing closer to God is one of the most frequent and powerful benefits cited by accountability partners. If you have a weak faith and want some help, accountability can be an outstanding tool to boost it. Be sure to discuss faith and other core values with your potential accountability partners to ensure that you are attaching the same significance to your accountability adventures.

Avon says accountability "is a means of achieving certain long-term goals. These goals will vary from person to person. For a Christian, it might mean wanting to grow closer to Jesus Christ. For the atheist, it might mean wanting to be a better contributor to society."

Gender and accountability groups

IN INTERVIEWING ACCOUNTABILITY PARTNERS, some general gender-related patterns emerge. Of course, any generalization along these lines is tenuous. At the same time, give gender at least a bit of consideration in your partner selection process.

Men may place a higher value on building discipline and personal power through conquering successively greater challenges. Women may place a higher value on the remarkable relationships they forge as they share successively more intimate parts of themselves and their lives.

Alexandra highlights a potential difference in how men and women view progress, "Men are more analytical about everything. They emphasize spreadsheets and can be more competitive. It's all about seeing progress through numbers. Women, in my experience, do not always need the numbers to see the progress another is making. We are more able to sense or intuit the progress in another, to hear it in her voice, or see it in her actions." Ideally, no group members will feel as though they are competing with each other, though it is a natural tendency—perhaps more so in males—to judge your performance relative to how your peers performed. Both men and women will experience greater peace of mind if they remember that performance is best measured against your previous self—and not against your fellow group members.

Another gender difference can emerge in how men and women critique each other. Men have relatively little difficulty saying, "You're getting fatter again; you'll probably want to bump up your exercise goals." My female accountability interviewees report that saying that to a woman is not nearly as easy! Men may be more harsh and direct with criticism and punishments, while women may be more compassionate and concerned with maintaining peaceful relationships. Kathleen also suggests it may be harder for women to fully divulge their faults.

Many times accountability group members commented that they could not share certain life elements in a mixed-gender context. Topics such as romance and sexuality can become trickier in a mixed-gender context. Thus, all my interviewees opted to have same-gender groups. Accountability within married couples is a key exception here as they already share their whole lives with each other.

Ideally, every accountability participant—male or female—will be able to provide both full feedback and full sharing. Some men could use an extra dose of compassion while some women may need an extra dose of candor. Great groups manage to avoid both being mean and holding back genuine feedback. Read the next chapter on confrontation for additional thoughts on criticizing appropriately.

Confrontation: pushing past the fear

SHARING WITH A GROUP raises novel tensions; you will naturally experience some apprehension associated with addressing unpleasant items in your accountability partners' lives. Recall that The Dudes called each other out on everything from messy rooms to binge drinking. This chapter contains some perspectives to help push past that resistance. Bear in mind that, as an accountability partner, you have particular responsibility to address such issues. These perspectives can also enrich relationships outside of accountability.

Often issues can stray into uncomfortable territory. Someone is engaging in some action that is persistently irksome, hurtful, or troubling. Such actions are ubiquitous in human relationships, but they elevate themselves to a tricky level when you feel hesitant to address those actions. Typical examples include addictive behaviors, unwise decisions, or disrespectful attitudes.

When confronted with these difficulties, you may wonder whether or not to address the matter. Internal dialogues can serve up innumerable reasons why you ought to remain silent. That dialogue usually sounds something like:

- We don't really go there.
- I don't want him to think that I'm uptight.
- That would make things awkward or uncomfortable.
- It won't really make a difference anyway.
- I think he knows; it will probably go away on its own.

Most reasons for silence bubble up in a context of fear. The brain, seeking a solution to the fearful notion of confrontation, gropes about for viable solutions to reinforce the silence while diminishing internal dissonance. However, these reasons usually do not justify silence.

Top-notch relationships are characterized by complete openness and trust. Failing to address trouble spots can impede the complete sharing which makes relationships great. I've come to believe that one should almost always address the issue—even though it's difficult. As such, below are some counter-arguments to short-circuit the temptations toward silence.

We don't really go there

Start! Venturing into untouched territories strengthens friendships. Have you ever surprised yourself and said, "Wow, I've never told that to anyone before!"? You feel surprised and delighted by the amount of trust and comfort that you have built up with that person in order to share at that level. Similarly, if few people have addressed the issue that you're dealing with, you develop a shared experience that enhances mutual trust.

I don't want him to think that I'm uptight

Your friend has formed and reinforced numerous positive impressions of you over the course of many hours shared together. It is exceedingly improbable that he would rapidly develop an unfavorable opinion about you based on a lone incident. It would be foolish to jump to such a conclusion. And, if he does, then you were otherwise doomed to have this poor judgment emerge at some point in the future.

That would make things awkward or uncomfortable

The sensations of awkwardness and discomfort are fleeting, while the benefits of your conversation can be life-changing. Sometimes you just need to bear down and rip off the bandage. When a patient is sick, a doctor does what is necessary to cure him. Treatment may require the patient swallowing peculiar chemical compounds, being sedated, getting undressed, having body hair removed, and/or getting sliced open. These processes are certainly awkward and uncomfortable! Nonetheless, they are required for recovery. Similarly, if your relationship is experiencing a form of sickness, you may need to engage in seemingly odd maneuverings to obtain a full recovery.

It really won't make a difference anyway

Excuse the heavy sarcasm for a moment as I speak to you on behalf of your friend: "Thank you for giving such consideration to me and my schedule. I appreciate you sparing me the eight minutes required to consider changing some harmful behavior. Furthermore, I'm amazed by your psychic foreknowledge that enables you to perfectly predict the course of action I will take on this issue." The choice to change a behavior is your friend's decision—not yours. By remaining silent, you rob him of the opportunity to make that choice.

I think he knows; it will probably go away on its own

A persistent issue, by its very nature, is probably not going to go away without some force intervening. Often that force is someone bringing up the topic. If not you, then who? All his other friends may either be unaware or uncomfortable addressing the issue. Unfortunately, most people don't have anyone in their lives to give the frank feedback necessary for improvement. You can witness these people on *American Idol*; they are the ones who embarrass themselves by singing very loudly, very poorly. No one ever told that poor person, "You should work on your pitch a bit before the audition." Friends don't let friends embarrass themselves on *American Idol*.

The ultimate underlying—albeit irrational—fear is that bringing up your concerns will somehow initiate a chain of events that will destroy your friendship as you know it. If having such a conversation would indeed create the ire or awkwardness that would somehow end your relationship, then your relationship was really doomed from the beginning. Issues will inevitably arise; if you can't tackle them, then things will fall apart. If your friend's unyielding character is destined to terminate your relationship, you may as well proactively conclude the relationship. There are billions of amazing humans on the earth and all-too-few hours to spend with them. Cycling through shallow relationships results in you spending more quality time with other people with whom you can engage in maximum, mutual enrichment.

The real question is not whether to address the issue, but how. I recommend the following approach:

- Plan the conversation in advance
- Reaffirm that you care
- Diplomatically ask caring questions
- Share observations rather than judgments
- Acknowledge your own shortcomings in that area
- Emphasize that these are just your perceptions—not the end all be all

A great way to open up such a conversation is to ask, "Would you prefer that I be generally pleasant and laughing all the time or directly challenge you to reach your potential?" That's also a great way to identify quality accountability partners.

The sandwich or Oreo approach is one useful feedback technique. Start with a positive statement, insert the negative statement, then reaffirm with a positive one. The way Jeremy challenged me to keep my room clean was a fine example. He told me that I was a man on a quest for optimality. He noted that my room did not support that quest. He emphasized how grace builds upon nature and encouraged me to give it a try. That goes over a lot better than saying, "You're a slob!" Now, if you use this technique frequently, people will catch onto you. They'll tune out the "bread" of your sandwich as they think, "Oh, boy here it comes." Also, make sure your positive statements are genuine instead of filler to employ the technique!

Meeting structure

IDEALLY, EACH ACCOUNTABILITY GATHERING will lavishly provide the support that each individual member requires— all at a leisurely pace. Unfortunately, your meetings will probably be shortened by the demands of life. It's important to settle upon a structure that members accept and that contributes to development in a time-effective manner. The structure of your meeting will evolve over time as you see what works well for your particular group of people.

As an initial example, recall that The Dudes settled upon the following structure:

1. General chit-chat and merriment as people roll in and get settled
2. Opening in prayer
3. Someone goes through the week's emotional highs and lows, victories, failures, noteworthy items, and overall score
4. The person "going" then passes the spreadsheet around to the others for visual scrutiny and commentary
5. Other members provide support, praise, admonishment, insight, and suggestions to the person who's "going"
6. The remaining members repeat steps 3 through 5
7. Execute celebrations and/or punishments (e.g. paying penalty dollars, performing pushups, etc.)
8. General pump up for the week ahead
9. Close in prayer

Such a structure emphasizes each individual and his performance on the week's objectives. If you're using a strong quantitative approach, it can be tempting to dive directly into the numbers, analyzing the patterns and bad days. Try to avoid such an immediate dive in order to better tackle the non-quantifiable stuff.

Other groups prefer to progress through a series of topics rather than a series of individuals. Such an approach may better facilitate connection and understanding of shared life experiences. Topic areas might include:

- Career
- Fitness
- Volunteering
- Spirituality
- Family
- Money
- Upcoming decisions
- Friendships
- Conflict and anger situations
- Stress
- Romance
- Nutrition

Find an applicable list of topics or use this long list to jog your memory about any major life events that you may forget about between the event and the meeting.

Other groups establish a revolving area of focus. It enables all of the members to focus on a single item together—then share their insights and reflections on the resolution after a week has elapsed. People engaging in this practice reported an increase in self-awareness and group unity.

Also give consideration to environmental factors. Rob says, "It's important for accountability groups to have a distinct meeting place to reinforce the idea that you're in a certain place for a certain reason, to be optimal!" Other groups like to set some mood music with pump up songs playing in the background.

Whatever your structure or location, make sure that you keep your meeting time sacred. Find a two-hour chunk and don't be shy about letting your members know that being twelve minutes tardy is unacceptable. Take a tip from Morgan, "Not meeting frequently will definitely make a group fall apart. So, we just set up a concrete time to meet once a week that everyone could attend…hold each other accountable for the meeting."

Also remember that the full accountability experience does not occur within the confines of the meetings. If the transformation process is relegated to the meeting sphere, it's easier to compartmentalize and miss out on maximum enrichment. Try to find opportunities to spend quality time with each other—particularly in the mutual pursuit of goals. Laura notes that their group does nighttime prayer together, while other groups work out as a crew. Connor says, "Guys have to hang out outside of the meetings to really develop that friendship. Some of the best conversations I have are walking to the gym or playing poker with my accountability men, not the meetings."

Lindsay provides three simple summary reminders: "If you don't have a set meeting time it can be hard. Also it is better when you see the other people in your group more often throughout the week so that you can remind each other of goals and track each other's progress. Also, have fun during meetings so that it is something to look forward to!"

Rules

ACCOUNTABILITY RELATIONSHIPS MAY BEGIN WITH trepidation. Clearly defining some operating norms can alleviate much of this tension. You may choose to have an informal arrangement or go all out and print, sign, and ratify your covenant. Potential rules for consideration include:

- **Confidentiality**. What's said in the group stays in the group—unless otherwise noted. The last thing anyone wants to encounter is an acquaintance greeting them with a, "So… I heard you're finally going to do something about your drinking problem." As Drew puts it, "I became so close to these men and developed an impenetrable bond with these men. Confessing all of your struggles and successes to these men with full confidence of their confidentiality is irreplaceable."[3]

- **Meeting times are sacred**. All members will do all that is in their power to honor the time of the group meetings. All will fight off scheduling marauders so that full attendance is possible.

- **Full engagement**. All parties will provide full attention to people as they are speaking. Any staring off in space or alternative distractions are to be avoided.

- **All for love**. Harsh words are reserved solely for corrective measures—not vengeance or blowing off steam. If you're on the receiving end of some infuriating feedback, just say "thank you." Feedback is a gift. Curtail the temptation to tell your gift-giver just where they can stick it!

- **Full expression**. Whenever a member of an accountability group feels she might have an inkling of potential corrective feedback, she's obligated to speak it. No restraints for fear of being offensive! Similarly, people will tell all about themselves.

- **Empathize and criticize**. Generally every failure is partially a person's lack of will and partially circumstances. Empathize with the circumstances and challenges, but criticize the failure of will. Give people credit where credit is due.

3. In case you were wondering…Yes, all my group members gave their consent to publish excerpts from our meetings. Thanks for watching out for confidentiality, though!

Reflections on the accountable lifestyle

ONE OF MY FAVORITE SPEAKERS and authors, Matthew Kelly, says, "The body is a wonderful servant, but a terrible master." The sensations of "I don't feel like it" all too frequently undermine our resolve. Mr. "I don't feel like it" frequently thwarts even the firmest of intentions. He is an elusive nemesis with many manifestations: I'm really tired. I'll do it tomorrow. I'm busy right now. I need to be up early tomorrow. I need to take advantage of this immediate opportunity. I have friends coming over...

The real transformation of The Dudes occurred not within the one- or two-hour meetings. Rather, it occurred in the ubiquitous moments of choice between our established goals and whimsical desires. The accountability meetings made the difference because they provided a powerful focus and incentive to choose the goal over the desires during all those moments. With time and focus, the force of will grows more powerful than the immediate desires. This growth is self-mastery.

This section is a peek inside what makes the prior accountability principles work. You can use it as a reference to answer your friends when they inquire, "Why are you so excited about this accountability thing?" The following pages will reflect on the moments of temptation and transformation that make the difference.

Where the rubber meets the road

Self-mastery is perhaps the most thrilling ability gained from accountability. We are bombarded by innumerable stimuli, opportunities, and temptations—each begging for additional attention. The TV says, "Watch me." The double cheeseburger says, "Eat me." The body says, "Let's hit the snooze." The dog says, "Play with me." Your friends say, "Let's hang out." Your significant other says,

"Call me." The pressures associated with these inducements are omnipresent. As a result, it can be quite easy to lose yourself in your immediate desires.

The accountability magic comes from having a handy counterweight to immediate desires. Jenny captures the struggle well; "I have grown excessively in my self-discipline. So many times I want to sleep instead of study, sleep instead of work out, sleep instead of pray, sleep instead of sending emails, or sleep instead of going to Mass. But stronger than my desire to sleep is my desire to tell my group that I got a 100%."

Articulating goals to others heightens their priority. Kathleen notes, "Having other people aware of my goals somehow makes them more real."

Anne Marie confirms, "It really commits you to doing something. Often I wouldn't have done something, but I did do it so I could check it off my accountability group goals." These moments occur often for accountability folks; we think of our groups nearly every time we have a desire to do what we shouldn't, or vice versa.

Having an initial boost helps start building the muscles of discipline. The capacity to say "no" increases and people reclaim control over what was previously controlling them. Reclaiming these personal faculties results in innumerable small—but glorious—personal victories that surprise the victors themselves. The results are exciting. For example, Chris reveals, "My most exciting victory was when I needed to pump out five more hours of studying in one night. I felt like this task was going to be impossible, but when I told myself that I needed to do this for the group, I sat down and didn't look back. The most gratifying thing was that I received an A on my test." Laura shares a similar incident: "The most exciting victory for me was waking up at 6:30 to work out five days a week. It was a very gratifying accomplishment every day to have worked out and showered by 8:15."

I just got a good pump

Weightlifters offer a useful perspective on decision-making whenever they comment on their "pumps" after a workout. They are referring to the sensation that usually follows a satisfying weight session wherein the lifter's muscles were thoroughly and healthily fatigued. Their muscles engorge with fluids and nutrients. The body feels enriched as it has risen to a challenge and a sensation of wakefulness enhances the rest of the day. The energizing experience provides pleasing after-effects. Weightlifters might sometimes call this a "good pump."

Every time a person deeply engages a part of his or her humanity, they experience a kind of pump. You can generate a good pump in many locations; it is not relegated to the confines of a gym. How would you describe the feeling immediately following a long dinner with a great friend you haven't seen in months? How about the sensation emerging after having thoroughly prepared for a presentation, to later dominate that challenge? What about the feeling after a lengthy, quiet session of prayer, reflection, or meditation? In all of these experiences, the sensations you experience in the hours afterwards feel deeply satisfying. Be it the thrill of personal victory or just a natural afterglow, just like the weightlifters, you got a good pump.

Now, contrast those sensations to how you usually feel immediately prior to engaging in such activities. It often occurs, in a moment of idle thought, that you should workout, schedule an appointment with a friend, prepare for that looming mental challenge, or spend some time in silence. Yet how often do we heed that thought? Most likely the answer is not enough. If such activities are so deeply satisfying, why do we neglect them? "I don't feel like it."

Doing what you feel like doing doesn't always lead you to choose richly satisfying activities. Your whims are not a reliable aid in decision-making; so try on a few different ones for size.

Matthew 7:16 offers a helpful thought: "You will know them by their fruits." Some of the wisest people who ever lived have observed that when they think about things of the material world they feel intense pleasure that fades, yet when they think about genuinely enriching human goods, the pleasure persists. To summarize: "I don't feel like it" is never an adequate reason to take (or not to take) any course of action.

Accountable people confirm that the thrill of victory is so much greater than the pleasures of doing what you feel like. Victories mount and the days in which you prioritize your tasks and decisions—as opposed to your immediate passions, desires, and opportunities—grow more and more frequent. Having a support group helps build momentum and liberates you from immediate desires. The donuts or video games suddenly don't seem quite so appealing. A group also increases your capacity to achieve any objective. This is true freedom. This is the joy of self-mastery.

An accountability mindset

Participants quickly discover that the mere presence of a little accountability—from any source—increases the probability that they will take particular actions. Making and fulfilling challenging commitments to your accountability partners builds the power of your word.

Rich describes the mindset that emerges: "You are constantly thinking in a group mentality. It is just not about yourself anymore." You have to answer to others. You may naturally desire to employ accountability in more and more opportunities to create bigger, more powerful commitments.

Whether or not you've got a group in place, if you want to make sure that you get something done, tell people about it! Perhaps your boss, mentor, family member, friends, or spouse. Tell whomever might resonate with your resolution. Tell the people who will follow up with you. You can integrate accountability in numerous small ways on a daily basis. Saying little things like, "I'll be going to the gym today after work" to your roommates or spouse will make them expect you later. If you fail to enact your small resolution, and show up directly after work, they will probably ask about it: "I thought you were going to the gym?" Many of these small exchanges integrated into your daily habits can serve to drastically improve performance on personal initiatives. The reason is that they are no longer personal initiatives, but rather living objectives. When commitments are shared with others, they become real. Your objectives now impact the world and you are responsible for them because you spoke them into reality.

The power of your word goes both ways. By regularly following up with all the people in your life, you can increase the likelihood that they will deliver on their commitments.

Farewell

Dearest reader,

I promised you "a wondrous adventure of friendship and self-mastery…with all the elation, fear, uncertainty, frustration, suspense, and joy of a literary masterpiece." Please hold me accountable to that.

Yes. That request is a bit of a sneaky trick. The only way you can hold me accountable to my promise is by taking a real crack at putting these principles into practice …and if you do that, you'll experience just what I've promised.

Several studies have found that very few book purchasers actually read past the first chapter of their new book. Even fewer actually do what the book recommends. You've already beaten the odds by finishing the book. So, finish the job in proving the numbers wrong. If you've read this whole book, it means you're intrigued. Find some people and do it! You won't regret it.

Finally, do let me know about the progress of your accountability adventure at www.teamupbook.com.

Keep it real.

Appendix: Spreadsheet formulas

IT'S NOT ESSENTIAL TO LEARN how to use spreadsheets for goal tracking, but they do offer a variety of advantages and flexibility. If you want to quickly implement software-aided goal-tracking, visit www.teamupbook.com for simple solutions and starter spreadsheets with explanatory comments. However, if you want to learn the underlying spreadsheet basics in an accountability context, read on.

Two of the most popular spreadsheet software programs available are Microsoft Excel and OpenOffice.org Calc. Excel is popular in the mainstream business community, so it might do well to practice it. If you don't have Excel on your computer, you can download OpenOffice for free at www.openoffice.org. Most of Calc's functions are identical to Excel's. You can download templates with handy instructional notes at www.teamupbook.com or just use the handy program to create your own worksheet online.

Excel

Excel spreadsheets are called "worksheets." You can create a new worksheet by pushing Ctrl + n. The little boxes formed by the gridlines are called "cells." If you start in the very top-most and left-most cell (i.e. "A1"), you can build a sample sheet by maneuvering around the cells and typing each formula listed in the sheet on the next page:

Goals	Swearing	Prayer	Exercise	Sleep	Reading
Total Occurrences Desired	7	21	6	7	7
Current Score	=SUM(B4: B10)/B2	=SUM(C4: C10)/C2	=SUM(D4: D10)/D2	=SUM(E4: E10)/E2	=SUM(F4: F10)/F2
01/01/2010					
=A4+1					
=A5+1					
=A6+1					
=A7+1					
=A8+1					
=A9+1					
		Overall	=AVERAGE(B3:F3)		

This worksheet adds the number of times a goal occurred during a week and divides it by the number of times desired. In Excel, you insert formulas by starting your statements with an "=" sign. Cell references have a letter and a number associated to them (e.g. "B4"). The letter represents the column, and the number represents the row. In B4 the "B" means the cell is in the 2nd column and "4" means the cell is in the 4th row. A range of cells is denoted by a colon in the middle. For example, the range "B4:B10" refers to a group of cells in column B, stretching from the 4th through the 10th rows.

You can insert a date by inputting it with typical slashes. Additionally, Excel's built-in numbering system allows you to add or subtract dates to numbers or other dates. The column on the left uses formulas to add one day to the previous day. The implication is that that you only have to input one day to establish all the dates for the week. Note how the +1 just means "plus one"

Similarly:

- *2 means "multiply by two"
- -2 means "subtract two"
- /2 means "divide by two"
- ^2 means "take to the second power"

Excel follows the typical order of operations that you learned in math class—Please Excuse My Dear Aunt Sally (PEMDAS). That is, it follows the sequence: Parentheses, then Exponents, followed by Multiplication/Division, and finally Addition/Subtraction. Throw in some parentheses if things seem off. For example typing "=(2+3)*7" into a cell would generate 35 while typing "=2+3*7" into a cell would generate 23).

Excel functions by using statements called…functions, which tell the numbers to do something. Handy functions for accountability are:

- =SUM displays the total from a series of cells. The example above calculates the current score for each goal by using the SUM function as well as the "/" sign to represent division. Combined, the formula adds up your points for a goal then divides it by the number of times that it happens. The result is your performance ratio (e.g. 50% of goal achieved).

- =AVERAGE takes the average (i.e. arithmetic mean) of a series of cells. Averaging your scores for all the goals will give you an overall score for the week.

- =NOW() inputs the current time. You can mingle this with other functions to create advanced pacing calculations.

Save your file (keyboard shortcut: Ctrl + s) in a prominent place like My Documents or your desktop. P.J. named his file "Excel-ence," which is a fine name for such a document.

If you want to get a little more advanced and incorporate a pace calculation, follow these steps below:

- Have one cell have the day starting the week in Excel's date format. On this example worksheet, that cell corresponds to A4.
- Create another cell with the current time by entering the function "=NOW()"into cell A11.
- Generate a fraction of how much your week has elapsed. If you count 7 days in your week, the denominator would be 7. So, in this example "=(A11-A4)/7" will give you the proportion of the week that has elapsed. Input this formula in B11. You may wish to label it by placing the text "elapsed" in a nearby cell.
- Excel will want to format this as a date, which will look weird. Click this odd-looking cell and format the number as a percentage (keyboard shortcut: Ctrl + Shift + 5). Now this cell clearly displays the percentage of the week elapsed (e.g. 50% has elapsed when you're exactly 3.5 days into the week).
- Now, your pace ratio is simply your overall score (D11 in this example) divided by the proportion of the week that has elapsed (B11 in this example). So, you can see you pace ratio in this example by typing the formula "=D11/B11" into a blank cell.

Bibliography and recommended resources

THESE SOURCES FORMED THE FOUNDATION of research underlying this book and/or nicely complement the accountability experience. For enhanced exploration of web and print sources, visit www.teamupbook.com.

Interviewees and informants

Asgedom, Mawi

Brummer, Anne Marie

Buenker, Jason

Byrne, Thomas

Butler, P.J.

Cummings, Christopher

Danstrom, Connor

Erickson, Buddy

Fernandes, Avon

Gelsthorpe, Laura

Graham, Kathleen

Hewitt, Jeremy

Holloway, Fr. Tom

Kale, Alexandra

Keane, Liz

Kempf, Robert

Landles-Dowling, Libbie

Malley, Katy

Marry, Kelly

Matsuhashi, Amy

Meyer, Jenny

Mitchell, Matt

Novak, Greg

Peterson, Drew

Pitcher, Jill

Schweighart, Rich

Shull, Lindsay

Smith, Kara

Stalcup, Chris

Vercimak, Jake

Whitman, Samantha

Zeeb, Morgan

Print resources

Allen, David. *Getting Things Done : The Art of Stress-Free Productivity.* New York: Penguin Books, 2003.

Aristotle. *Ethics.* Oxford, Mississippi: Project Gutenberg, 2005.

Breus, Michael Ph.D., *Beauty Sleep: Look Younger, Lose Weight, and Feel Great Through Better Sleep.* New York: Plume, 2007

Cooper, Robert K. *The Other 90%: How to Unlock Your Vast Untapped Potential for Leadership and Life.* New York: Three Rivers Press, 2001.

Ferrazzi, Keith. *Who's Got Your Back? The Breakthrough Program to Build Deep, Trusting Relationships That Create Success—and Won't Let You Fail.* New York: Broadway Books, 2009.

Franklin, Benjamin. *The Autobiography of Benjamin Franklin.* Edited by Charles W Elliot LLD. New York: P F Collier & Son Company, 1909.

Handley, Rob. *Character Counts: A Guide for Accountability Groups.* Grand Island, Nebraska: Cross Training Publishing, 1999.

Hill, Napoleon. *Think and Grow Rich.* Radford, VA: Wilder Publications, 2007.

Hustad, Megan. *How to be Useful.* New York: Houghton Mifflin, 2008.

Kelley, Sarano. *The Game.* San Diego: Sarano Kelley, Inc., 2001.

Kelly, Matthew. *The Rhythm of Life: Living Every Day with Passion and Purpose.* New York: Fireside, 2004.

Lehrer, Jonah. *"Don't! The secret of self-control."* New Yorker, May 18, 2009.

Riedweg, Christoph. *Pythagoras: His Life, Teaching, and Influence.* Translated by Steven Rendall. Ithaca, New York: Cornell University Press, 2005.

Websites

www.43things.com

www.aa.org/bigbookonline

www.baycongroup.com

www.comotivate.com

www.goalforit.com

www.goalmigo.com

www.goaltribe.com

www.joesgoals.com

www.mecanbe.com

www.mint.com

www.myfooddiary.com

www.nike.com

www.openoffice.org

www.peertrainer.com

www.revolutionhealth.com

www.sparkpeople.com

www.stickk.com

www.teamupbook.com

www.thedailyplate.com

www.thinkexist.com

Index

A

a little help from your friends *15, 17–26, 89*
See also SETTING GOALS

a perfect day *88*
See also SETTING GOALS

apologize *63*

arguments *42, 47, 63*

Aristotle *113*

B

balance *17–18, 42, 86*
See also SETTING GOALS

blasts of inspiration *88*
See also SETTING GOALS

boss *1, 14, 15, 26, 27, 29, 30, 34, 72, 91, 97, 144*
See also SOMEONE WATCHING

bottlenecks *17, 18, 22, 26, 42*
See also SETTING GOALS

C

calling your shot *36, 51–52, 111*
See also TRACKING PERFORMANCE

cash money *43, 54, 109*
See also INCENTIVES AND PUNISHMENTS

check-ins *27, 53, 112*
See also TRACKING PERFORMANCE

Connor *7–10, 11–12, 13–16, 17–26, 27–32, 33–40, 41–44, 45–46, 47–50, 51–56, 57–58, 59–62, 63–64, 65–70, 71, 85, 108, 125, 137*

H

harsh words *29–30, 109, 129–130*
  See also INCENTIVES AND PUNISHMENTS

Hill, Napoleon *78*

HOBY *39*

hydration *23, 41, 48, 91–92*

I

incentives and punishments *32, 37–40, 43, 107–110*
  cash money *43, 54, 109*
  dares *109*
  food and beverage *107*
  harsh words *29–30, 109, 129–130*
  main event, the *37, 53, 108*
  physical challenge *37, 108*
  pushups *37, 38, 39, 41, 86, 105, 107, 108, 135*
  self-denial *109*
  slow clap, the *38, 53, 108*
  Steak n Shake *32, 37, 38, 43, 52, 53, 54, 73*
  verbal kudos *28, 29, 30, 33–35, 107*
  victory dance *53, 108*
Internet *79, 102, 116–118*
  Facebook *117*
  ShoutNow *117*
  stickK *79, 117*
  Twitter *117*

J

Jeremy *13–16, 17–26, 27–32, 33–40, 41–44, 47–50, 51–56, 57–58, 59–62, 63–64, 65–70, 73, 123, 134*

R

Return On Energy *87*
> *See also* SETTING GOALS

rewards
> *See* INCENTIVES AND PUNISHMENTS

Robbins, Anthony *86*

Rocky *9*

ROE
> *See* RETURN ON ENERGY

S

scheduling *35–36, 112*
> *See also* TRACKING PERFORMANCE

Schwarzenegger, Arnold *17*

scripture *24, 144*
> *See also* FAITH

self-denial *109*
> *See also* INCENTIVES AND PUNISHMENTS

self-mastery *2–3, 25, 54–55, 87, 141–142*
> *See also* SETTING GOALS
> *See also* MARSHMALLOW TEST

setting goals *15, 17–26, 42, 57–58, 61, 74–76, 83–95, 143–144*
> a little help from your friends *15, 17–26, 89*
> a perfect day *88*
> balance *17–18, 42, 86*
> blasts of inspiration *88*
> bottlenecks *17, 18, 22, 26, 42*
> liberation *87*
> Return On Energy *87*
> self-mastery *25, 54–55, 87, 141–142*
> shoulds *24, 24–25, 86*
> top-down *87–88*
> visualization *48, 111*

S (cont.)

T

T (cont.)